WHAT AFTER SCHOOL?

WHAT AFTER SCHOOL?

Self Explanatory Guide to help you plan your Career

VISHAL MALIK

PARTRIDGE
A Penguin Random House Company

To order additional copies of this book, contact
Partridge India
000 800 10062 62
www.partridgepublishing.com/india
orders.india@partridgepublishing.com

CONTENTS

ABOUT THE AUTHOR

Vishal Malik is born in India on July 08, 1980 and is grown up in Yamunanagar in the state of Haryana. He completed his studies till graduation in Yamunanagar. After that, he moved to Rohtak town for doing his post-graduation studies. He was always in the list of toppers during his academics. He pursued doctorate degree to continue his studies.

Author has a vast professional experience of working for 10 years in big organizations at reputed positions. He worked for the companies like Tata Consultancy Services, COLT Technologies, Oracle Corporation, Mindtree Consulting and Avantha Technologies during these 10 years. He visited numerous locations in India and overseas during this time.

Author has a strong interest in providing guidance to students and professionals. Thousands of students and professionals took the benefit of guidance skills of author and became successful in their personal and professional life.

ACKNOWLEDGEMENT

What, After School? This question comes in the mind of every student during his/ her studies in school. I have tried to help students in planning their professional career in this book. This book will help the students to look in to their own personality and will help them choose suitable career paths.

I am thankful to all the students who met me in last many years for queries about their career and repeatedly chased me for providing them the material for their career planning in the form of a complete book. I am also thankful to my wife for her sacrifices to help me bring this dream of students into reality.

The information about the courses, provided in this book has been gathered from various known and unknown sources. The details are written after conducting various seminars, meetings, interviews and discovering the information from other sources. The information provided in this book is latest and up to date but the readers should keep in mind that change is the only constant thing in this world. There might be some new course available in the market that is not mentioned in this book and there is a little possibility of having some outdated courses as well. Anyways, the main aim of this book is to help students to know their personality and discover which career suits them best. I have tried my best to provide such a material that no one will be disappointed after reading this book.

Again, I give thanks to all the persons who helped me directly or indirectly in writing this book. Also I would like to get any suggestions on improvements for future editions of this book on e-mail ID komallearningsolutions@ gmail.com

WARM UP TIPS

It's choice, not chance, that determines your destiny—Jean Nidetch

Learning is a never ending process in our life. We start learning from the moment we take birth and keep it on till we die. We learn from our parents, teachers, friends, relatives, neighbours, colleagues and from strangers as well. We learn from good as well as from bad experiences of life. We learn from human beings, nature and manmade machines. Although we keep on learning during all our life, yet there is a special importance of school education in our life. All lucky kids go to school for formal education starting from pre-nursery, then kinder garten, primary, middle, higher and senior secondary level.

Life of a student comes to a turning point once his formal school education completes. Most of students are not well prepared for this turn. They spend around 15 years in school but do not give a single day to think about what they are going to do after school. If few of them do so, they do not do it in a proper way. The turn goes well if the career path is properly selected according to your skills, interests, personality and aptitude level. The turn, if taken wrong, results in dis-satisfaction, failures and lifetime frustration. The turn, if taken wrong, can't be reversed in all your life.

Therefore, you should think about what, after school, while you are in school. You should sit back, hold yourself for some time and decide where you are planning to go.

The world is all full of opportunities and you are full of skills and talents. The almighty God has not created anything useless in this world. Therefore, never under-estimate yourself and always try to find the special god gifted talents in you. Give some time to discover yourself, know your abilities, interests, develop your skills and then decide on your future career path. This process does not take months and years, it is just to re-invent you and few days will be Ok if you are doing it by yourself without any guidance. With proper guidance, one single day or few hours would be enough to get an initial evaluation report for you. You should choose your career wisely according to the evaluation report generated by you or your career guide.

There are seven points that you should keep in mind while deciding about your career:

1. Never follow the crowd
2. Match your career with your skills and talents
3. Match your career with your personality and the working style you like
4. Ask your friends and family about what option suits you
5. Never forget your interests and priorities
6. Think twice before taking risk
7. Ask yourself—How much you can sacrifice for this career option?

KNOW THE OPTIONS

When you know better you do better—Maya Angelou

There are uncountable career opportunities in this world and all of these require persons with different skills and talents. The first step to plan about your career is to grab the knowledge about maximum of these available opportunities. This step needs a deep investigation of the current career options available around the globe. A thorough understanding and vast knowledge of available opportunities will create more options for you to choose from.

There are three categories of school students based on their broad view about their career.

- School students who are planning to complete their higher/senior secondary education and like to go for a job/business (First kind of students)
- School students who are planning to do some vocational course after their higher/senior secondary education and like to go for a job/business (Second kind of students)
- School students who are planning to study further after their higher/senior secondary education and like to build a strong career of their choice (Third kind of students)

The first kind of students are generally not much serious about the choices or options. Anyways, there are various choices available for this kind of students as well. This type of students can try for various job openings from government departments, private and public sector companies. They can go for their own business as well. Some of the options available for these kinds of students are listed as:

- Accountant
- Assistant
- Attendant

- Constable
- Driver
- Fireman
- Guard
- Lower division clerk
- Mechanic
- Operator
- Receptionist
- Stenographer
- Technician
- Tele-caller

The second kind of students also has various choices for certificate/vocational courses after school. They can go for ITI courses, Polytechnic courses, Diploma courses, Trainings and other certificate courses available from various government and non-government institutions.

ITI and other short term courses

ITI (Industrial Training Institute) and ITC (Industrial Training Centre) in India provide technical trainings through a big list of courses to students. The basic qualification required for these courses is matriculation. The main aim of these institutes is to provide trained manpower to industries for various technical fields. Some of the career choices available for students pursuing these institutes are:

- Animation
- Apparel design
- Architectural assistant
- Automobile technology
- Bakery and confectionary
- Beauty and fitness
- Computer hardware
- Cosmetology
- Cyber law
- Dairy technology
- Data entry
- Dental laboratory technician
- Draughtsman mechanic
- Dress making
- Driving
- Electrician

- Electronic mechanic
- Event management assistant
- Fibre optic technology
- Fire and safety
- Food processing
- Footwear and leather technology
- Fruits and vegetable processing
- Hair designing
- House keeping
- Instrument mechanic
- Interior decoration and designing
- Jewellery designing
- Lift technology
- Marketing and sales
- Meat technology
- Mobile phone repairing
- Office management
- Photography
- Plastic processing
- Pre-school management
- Radio and TV mechanic
- Refrigeration and AC mechanic
- Restaurant services
- Retail management
- Screen printing
- Tool and die making
- Tractor mechanic
- Travel and tourism
- Welding technology

Paramedical Courses

A paramedic is an expert who provides support and assistance to doctors for improved diagnosis and therapy. Trained professionals in this field are in high demand these days in India and overseas. Various courses are available in this field from many reputed institutes and colleges. Some of the options available for students with qualification of Xth or XII are:

- Dialysis technology
- Health inspection
- Laboratory technology
- Nursing

- Operation theatre technology
- Ophthalmic technology
- X-ray technology

Polytechnic Courses

Polytechnic is a reputed technical training institute in India that offers 3 year diploma courses in engineering. The basic qualification required for these courses is Xth. Students can get a supervisor or junior engineer job after completing this course. Some of the choices available for students are:

- Aeronautical engineering
- Agricultural engineering
- Apparel design engineering
- Architecture engineering
- Automobile engineering
- Bio-medical engineering
- Bio-technology
- Business administration
- Ceramic technology
- Chemical engineering
- Civil engineering
- Computer science engineering
- Electrical engineering
- Electronic and Communication
- Electronic engineering
- Fashion technology
- Handloom technology
- Industrial engineering
- Instrumentation technology
- Interior decoration
- Library science
- Marine engineering
- Mechanical engineering
- Production engineering
- Telecommunication engineering
- Textile technology

The third kind of students are more serious about their career choice and want to build a successful career of their choice. They opt to go for higher studies.

There are mainly three streams you have to choose from, after Xth and that are Science, Arts and Commerce. Science stream can further be sub-divided based on three types of career options available namely Engineering, Medical and other Science careers.

Different career opportunities are available under every stream and we cannot give more weightage to one over another as all these opportunities fit to persons with different skills and talents. A person who has the skills and talent to be an actor cannot fit himself in banking or engineering. Even if he makes this wrong choice, he will not be happy in such professions. In the same way, if a person has skills to be a top engineer or doctor will not be happy and successful if given a career of accountant, lawyer or any other field.

Science Stream

Science stream have a reputation of known as best out of all three streams since it is preferred by most of the topper students. The subjects include Physics, Chemistry, Mathematics and Biology. There is an option to take Mathematics or Biology or Both. The combination of these subjects excluding biology is referred as Non-Medical (or PCM) and the combination of these subjects excluding mathematics is referred as Medical (or PCB). Various careers in this stream are explained here.

Engineering Careers

The choices and opportunities available in Engineering are countless and are in high demand these days. The minimum qualification required for engineering is XII or equivalent with good marks having subjects Physics, Chemistry and Mathematics. There are many colleges, institutions and universities offering engineering courses to students. Many of these give admission based on ranking in entrance test and also need a minimum qualification. On the other side, many of these are giving admissions to students without taking any entrance test. Choosing a proper institution for course is a different matter and that too require a deep investigation. Some of the choices available under this career field are:

Aeronautical Engineering
Area of work

- Design, Develop and Test aircrafts, space vehicles, surface effect vehicles, missiles and related component systems

- Design and Develop commercial, military, executive, general aviation, special purpose aircraft, space vehicles, satellites, missiles and related hardware
- Test models, prototypes and production vehicles to study and evaluate their operational characteristics
- May specialize in design and development of structural components
- May specialize in analytical programs concerned with ground or flight testing, development of acoustic, thermodynamic or propulsion systems
- May assist in planning technical phases of air transportation systems or other aspects of flight operations, maintenance or logistics

Scope

- Domestic and International Airlines
- Government owned aircraft service/manufacturing unit
- Civil Aviation
- DRDO, NASA, ISRO
- National Aeronautical Lab

Agriculture Engineering
Area of work

- Observe environmental problems and consult with contractors to monitor construction activities
- Test agricultural machinery and equipment to ensure adequate performance
- Design structures for crop storage, animal shelter, animal and crop processing and supervise their construction
- Provide advice on issues related to pollution management, river control and ground and surface water resources
- Conduct educational programs that provide farmers or farm cooperative members with information that can help them improve agricultural productivity
- Design food processing plants and related mechanical systems
- Supervise food processing or manufacturing plant operations
- Plan and direct construction of rural electric-power distribution systems and irrigation, drainage and flood control systems
- Prepare reports, sketches, working drawings, specifications, proposals and budgets for proposed sites or systems

- Meet with clients such as district or regional councils, farmers and developers to discuss their needs
- Design sensing, measuring, and recording devices and other instrumentation used to study plant or animal life

Scope

- Agricultural Co-operators
- Bio-processing Industries
- Farming companies
- Fertilizers and Irrigation companies
- Food Processing Industries
- Forestry
- Large farms and Estate
- Agricultural Equipment Manufacturers
- NGOs
- Mining and Rehabilitation

Architectural Engineering
Area of work

- Construction management of new structures
- Renovation and consolidation of existing structures
- Work with team of engineers and architects
- Design and analysis of heating, ventilating and air conditioning systems
- Efficiency and design of plumbing, fire protection and electrical systems
- Acoustic and lighting planning
- Provide any failure coping mechanisms
- Reinforcement of structural designs

Scope

- Construction related industries
- Architectural firms and companies
- Government agencies responsible for renovating and preserving ancient/historical structures
- House movers and planning bodies
- Structural consultants
- Hazard control and rehabilitation agencies

Atmospheric Oceanic Science and Technology
Area of work

- Study of undersea volcanoes and their link to plate tectonics
- Study how changes in Earth's continents affected ancient climates
- Analyse and record oceanographic and meteorological data to forecast changes in weather or sea condition
- Sketch surface weather charts, upper air charts, sea condition charts, and other charts and maps to indicate weather and sea conditions
- Prepare and forecast warnings of severe and hazardous weather and sea conditions
- Perform preventative maintenance on meteorological and oceanographic equipment
- Investigate chemical and physical atmospheric properties encompassing natural processes, perturbations, and assessment of future conditions
- Atmospheric processes in the polar environment

Scope

- Ocean life preservation agencies
- Weather analyst
- University professor
- Tsunami analyst
- Researcher in marine biology

Automobile Engineering
Area of work

- Develop improved or new designs for automotive structures, engines, transmissions and associated automotive equipments
- Modify existing equipments on production vehicles
- Direct building, modification, and testing of vehicles using computerized work aids
- Conduct experiments and tests on existing designs and equipments to obtain data on function and performance of equipments
- Analyse data to develop new designs for motors, chassis, and other related mechanical, hydraulic, and electro-mechanical components and systems in automotive equipments

- Design components and systems to provide maximum customer value and vehicle function, including improved economy and safety of operation, control of emissions, and operational performance, at optimum costs
- Direct and coordinate building or modification of automotive equipment or vehicle to ensure conformance with engineering design
- Direct testing activities on components and equipments under designated conditions to ensure operational performance meets design specifications
- Alter or modify design to obtain specified functional and operational performance
- May assist in developing structural design for auto body
- May conduct research studies to develop new concepts in automotive engineering field

Scope

- Automobile Manufacturing Industry
- Maintenance and Service stations
- Private Transport Companies
- Defence Services and Establishments
- Faculty jobs in universities

Bio-chemical Engineering and Bio-technology
Area of work

- Deal with design and construction of unit processes that involve biological organisms or molecules such as bio-reactors
- Study chemical processes of living organisms
- Conduct research to determine action of foods, drugs, serums, hormones, and other substances on tissues and vital processes of living organisms
- Analyse and identify hormones, vitamins, allergens, minerals, and enzymes and determines effects on body functions
- Examine chemical aspects of formation of antibodies and conduct research into chemistry of cells and blood corpuscles
- Study chemistry of living processes, such as mechanisms of development of normal and abnormal cells, breathing and digestion, and of living energy changes, such as growth, aging, and death

- Clean, purify, refine, and prepare pharmaceutical compounds for commercial distribution and develop new drugs and medications
- Perform qualitative and quantitative chemical analysis of body fluids and exudates to provide information used in diagnosis and treatment of diseases
- Test specimens, such as urine, blood, spinal fluid, and gastric juices for presence and quantity of sugar, albumin, drugs, toxins and blood gases such as oxygen
- Develop mathematical models to simulate human bio-behavioural systems in order to obtain data for measuring or controlling life processes
- Design and develop instruments and devices such as artificial organs, cardiac pacemakers and ultrasonic imaging devices

Scope

- Consult with chemists or biologists to develop or evaluate novel technologies
- Medical researcher
- Pharmaceutical companies
- Food Technologist
- Toxicologist
- Technical Brewer
- Energy Engineer

Bio-medical Engineering
Area of work

- Application of engineering principles and design concepts to medicine and biology
- Research and development
- Development of biocompatible prostheses, diagnostic and therapeutic medical devices ranging from clinical equipment to micro-implants, common imaging equipment such as MRIs and EEGs
- Conduct research into biological aspects of humans or animals to develop new theories and facts
- Design life-support apparatus
- Utilize principles of engineering and bio-behavioural sciences to plan and conduct research concerning behavioural, biological, psychological or other life systems
- Study engineering aspects of bio-behavioural systems of humans

- Develop mathematical models to simulate human bio-behavioural systems in order to obtain data for measuring or controlling life processes
- Design and develop instruments and devices such as artificial organs, cardiac pacemakers and ultrasonic imaging devices capable of assisting medical or other health-care personnel in observing, repairing or treating physical ailments or deformities
- May specialize in design and development of biomedical equipment used by medical facilities and is known as Clinical Engineer

Scope

- Ergonomic Specialist
- Molecular Biology
- Radiology Technician
- Cardiac Technologist
- Human Factors Analyst
- Biomedical Instrumentation Technician

Bio-resource Engineering
Area of work

- Work on Thermo-chemical conversion technologies and Bio-chemical conversion technologies
- Plan and participate in activities concerned with study, development and inspection of solid-waste resource recovery systems and marketability of solid-waste recovery products
- Conduct studies of chemical and mechanical solid-waste recovery processes and system designs to evaluate efficiency and cost-effectiveness of proposed operations
- Inspect solid-waste resource recovery facilities to determine compliance with regulations governing construction and use
- Collect data on resource recovery systems and analyse alternate plans to determine most feasible systems for specific solid-waste
- On-site land treatment
- Handling of organic waste
- Design of ecological systems to meet certain human and non-human needs
- Study of water and soil for watershed analysis, irrigation and drainage plans

- Design of machinery components that will shape the future of agriculture

Scope

- Agricultural firms and industries
- Mining industries
- Oil and gas companies
- Environmental project planners for government
- Professional agrologist
- Bio-fuel manufacturing industry
- Food processing industry

Ceramic Engineering
Area of work

- Conduct research, design machinery, develop processing techniques and direct technical work concerned with manufacturing of ceramic products
- Direct testing of physical, chemical and heat-resisting properties of materials such as clay and silica
- Analyse results of test to determine combinations of materials which will improve quality of products
- Conduct research into methods of processing, forming, and firing of clay to develop new ceramic products, such as ceramic machine tools, refractories for space vehicles, and for use in glass and steel furnaces
- Design equipment and apparatus for forming, firing and handling products
- Coordinate testing activities of finished products for characteristics such as texture, colour, durability, glazing and refractory properties
- May specialize in one branch of ceramic production such as brick, glass, crockery, tile, pipe or refractories
- May specialize in developing heat-resistant and corrosion-resistant materials for use in aerospace, electronics and nuclear energy fields

Scope

- Indian space research organization (ISRO)
- Defence metallurgical research laboratory

- Bhabha Atomic Research Centre
- Plasma Research Centre
- Research Work and development
- Ceramics technology expert
- Space research organizations

Chemical Engineering
Area of work

- Design equipments and develop processes for manufacturing chemicals and related products
- Conduct research to develop new and improved chemical manufacturing processes
- Design, plan layout, and oversee workers engaged in constructing, controlling, and improving equipment to carry out chemical processes
- Analyse operating procedures and equipment and machinery functions to reduce processing time and cost
- Design equipment to control movement, storage and packaging of solids, liquids and gases
- Design and plan measurement and control systems for chemical plants based on data collected in laboratory experiments and pilot plant operations
- Determine most effective arrangement of unit operations such as mixing, grinding, crushing, heat transfer, size reduction, hydrogenation, distillation, purification, oxidation, polymerization, evaporation and fermentation
- Direct activities of workers who operate and control equipment as condensers, absorption and evaporation towers, kilns, pumps, stills, valves, tanks, boilers, compressors, grinders, pipelines, electro-magnets and centrifuges to effect required chemical or physical change
- Perform tests and take measurements throughout stages of production to determine degree of control over variables such as temperature, density, specific gravity and pressure
- May apply principles of chemical engineering to solve environmental problems
- May apply principles of chemical engineering to solve bio-medical problems

- May develop electro-chemical processes to generate electric currents using controlled chemical reactions or to produce chemical changes, using electric currents
- May specialize in heat transfer and energy conversion, petrochemicals and fuels, materials handling, pharmaceuticals, foods, forest products or products such as plastics, detergents, rubber or synthetic textiles

Scope

- Chemical process industry
- Nuclear energy
- Material science
- Food production
- Medicine industry
- Cosmetic industry
- Fertilizer producers

Civil Engineering
Area of work

- Plan, design and direct civil engineering projects such as roads, railroads, airports, bridges, harbours, channels, dams, irrigation systems, pipelines and power plants
- Analyse reports, maps, drawings, blueprints, tests and aerial photographs on soil composition, terrain, hydrological characteristics and other topographical and geological data to plan and design project
- Calculate cost and determine feasibility of project based on analysis of collected data
- Prepare or direct preparation and modification of reports, specifications, plans, construction schedules, environmental impact studies and designs for project
- Inspect construction site to monitor progress and ensure conformance to engineering plans, specifications and construction and safety standards
- May direct construction and maintenance activities at project site
- Conduct material testing and analysis using tools and equipment and applying engineering knowledge necessary to conduct tests
- Prepare reports on tests conducted and their results
- Survey project sites to obtain and analyse topographical details of sites using maps and surveying equipment

- Draft detailed dimensional drawings such as those needed for highway plans, structural steel fabrication and water control projects
- Calculate dimensions, profile specifications and quantities of materials such as steel, concrete and asphalt
- Inspect construction site to determine conformance of site to design specifications

Scope

- Project manager
- Senior estimator
- Design engineer
- Proposal engineer
- Highway construction supervisor
- Government contractor
- Construction consultant
- Site engineer

Clinical Engineering
Area of work

- Deal with actual implementation of medical equipments and technologies used in hospitals and other clinical settings
- Bio-medical Equipment Technicians (BMET)
- Deal with selection of technological products/services and their logistical management
- Work with government regulators on inspections/audits
- Collaborate with medical device producers for advice on improvement or devising new products
- Test equipment such as walking aids, wheelchairs and speech synthesizers
- Work on making artificial joints, heart valves and hearing implants from new materials to lessen the chance of rejection by the patient's body
- Work on designing equipments that allow doctors to try new medical techniques, for example, optical instruments for keyhole surgery and image-guided surgery
- Day-to-day management of medical equipment, such as scanners, imaging machines and monitoring systems
- Carry out quality assurance checks to ensure all equipment is working correctly and safely

Scope

- Research management
- Clinical network technician
- Clinical modelling
- Clinical system analyst
- Government regulatory agencies

Coastal Engineering
Area of work

- Deal with conservation, development and exploitation of the coastline and coastal resources
- Investigate, design and perform civil construction from the limit of the continental shelf

Scope

- Coastal resource analyst
- Fishery industries
- Coast-guard technician/associate
- Government research bodies
- Coastal organic life analyst

Computational Science and Engineering
Area of work

- Deal with development and application of computational models and simulations
- Deal with high performance computing
- Deal with solving complex physical problems arising in engineering analysis and design
- Diverse application in fields like:

  - o   mechanical engineering
  - o   aerospace engineering
  - o   biology and medicine
  - o   civil engineering
  - o   computer engineering
  - o   electrical and telecommunication engineering
  - o   industrial engineering
  - o   material science

- o   nuclear engineering
- o   petroleum engineering
- o   numerical weather predictions
- o   battlefield simulations
- o   astrophysical systems
- o   transportation
- o   computational geophysics
- o   military gaming

Scope

- Defence services
- Almost every industry has a job for this major
- Record analyst

Computer Science Engineering
Area of work

- Software development
- Hardware engineering
- System design
- System analyst
- Network engineering
- Database administration
- Web development
- Video game development

Scope

- IT sector
- MNC's
- E-commerce specialist
- Software manufacturers
- Universities
- Government institutes and agencies
- Banks

Construction Engineering and Management
Area of work

- Designing, planning, construction and management of infrastructures such as highways, bridges, airports, railroads, buildings, dams and utilities
- Work as an interface between civil engineers and construction managers
- Learn designing aspects much like civil engineers and construction site management functions much like construction managers

Scope

- Project manager
- Design engineer
- Proposal engineer
- Highway construction supervisor
- Government contractor
- Construction consultant
- Site engineer

Control and Automation
Area of work

- Design and draft systems of electrical, hydraulic and pneumatic control for machines and equipments such as arc welders, robots, conveyors and programmable controllers
- Design and draft arrangement of linkage of conductors, relays, and other components of electrical, electronic, hydraulic, pneumatic and lubrication devices using drafting tools
- Diagram logic system for functions such as sequence and timing control
- Design and draft diagrams of cable connection for robots, robot end-of-arm tool, robot controller and other machines
- Illustrate and describe installation and maintenance details
- Confer with assembler and wirer, industrial equipment to resolve problems regarding building of controls systems
- Review schematics with customer's representatives to answer questions during installation of robot systems

- Observe gauges during trial run of programmed machine and equipment operation to verify that electrical signals in system conform to specifications
- May design controls for energy conversion or other industrial plant monitoring systems
- May use computer and software programs to produce design drawings
- Automated mining
- Automated video surveillance
- Automated highway systems
- Automated waste management
- Automated manufacturing
- Home automation
- Industrial automation
- Agent-assisted Automation

Scope

- CAD designer
- Automation Control Designer
- Automation Development Personnel
- Global Process Coordinator in large automated plants
- Industries involving large automated systems for manufacturing
- Electricity Boards
- Large Scale Industries
- Manufacturing Plants
- Power Corporations
- Hydro-Electricity sector

Corrosion Engineering
Area of work

Corrosion engineering deal with application of scientific knowledge, natural laws and physical resources to design and implement materials, structures, devices, systems and procedures to manage the natural phenomenon of corrosion

Scope

- Oil refineries
- Chemical plants
- Iron/metal processing industry

- Government regulatory authority and inspection
- Monumental Inspection
- Construction Analyst

Design Engineering
Area of work

- Design engineering is a general term that covers multiple engineering disciplines including electrical, mechanical, industrial design, civil engineering and architectural engineering
- Take care of the total system as well as inner working and engineering of a design
- Work with a team of engineers and designers to develop the conceptual, preliminary and detail design and the most critical parts
- Develop product concepts and specifications
- Direct the design effort
- Deal with complex technological and scientific systems like aircraft, spacecraft, rockets, trains, ships, dams, bridges, building structures, urban infrastructure, machinery, production systems, propulsion systems, oil, gas etc
- Deal with mining exploration systems, manufacturing processes, military systems, cars, electronics, computers, power generation systems and power distribution systems
- Concerned with designing a new product or system
- Compile data, compute quantities, determine materials needed and prepare cost estimates

Scope

- Structural designer
- Fabricator
- Erector
- Dimension consultancy
- Design simulation departments
- Site/structural planners for government projects

Earthquake Engineering
Area of work

- Protecting society, the natural and the man-made environment from earthquakes by limiting the seismic risk to socio-economically acceptable levels
- Foresee the potential consequences of strong earthquakes on urban areas and civil infrastructure
- Design, construct and maintain structures to perform at earthquake exposure up to the expectations and in compliance with building codes
- Study and interpret seismic data to locate earthquakes and earthquake faults
- Review, analyse, and interpret data from seismographs and geophysical instruments
- Establish existence and activity of faults and direction, motion and stress of earth movements before, during and after earthquakes
- Conduct research on seismic forces affecting deformative movements of earth
- May issue maps or reports indicating areas of seismic risk to existing or proposed construction or development

Scope

- Seismology institutes
- Government jobs
- Earthquake awareness programs
- Structural engineer
- Rehabilitation expert

Electrical Engineering
Area of work

- Research, develop, design and test electrical components, equipments and systems for commercial, industrial and domestic purposes
- Develop applications of controls, instruments and systems for new commercial, domestic and industrial uses
- Direct activities to ensure manufacturing, construction, installation and operational testing conform to functional specifications and customer requirements

- May direct and coordinate operation, maintenance and repair of equipment and systems in field installations
- May use computer-assisted engineering and design software and equipment to perform engineering tasks

Scope

- Design Industries
- Production plants
- Natural gas plants
- Petroleum
- Steel plants
- Chemical plants
- Indian Railways
- Armed forces (Technical Branch)
- Thermal and nuclear power corporation
- Electricity Boards
- Large Scale Industries
- Manufacturing Plants
- Power Corporations
- Hydro-Electricity sector

Electrical Engineering (power)
Area of work

- Design power system facilities and equipments
- Coordinate construction, operation and maintenance of electric power generating, receiving and distribution stations, transmission lines and distribution systems and equipments
- Design and plan layout of generating plants, transmission and distribution lines, and receiving and distribution stations
- Prepare drawings of specific type of equipment and materials to be used in construction and equipment installation
- Estimate labour, material, construction and equipment costs
- Inspect completed installations for conformance with design and equipment specifications and safety standards
- Observe operation of installation for conformance with operational standards
- Coordinate operation and maintenance activities to ensure optimum utilization of power system facilities and meet customer demands for electrical energy

Scope

- Indian Railways
- Armed forces (Technical Branch)
- Thermal and nuclear power corporation
- Electricity Boards
- Large Scale Industries
- Manufacturing Plants
- Power Corporations
- Hydro-Electricity sector

Energy and Environmental Engineering
Area of work

- Inspect homes of utility company customers to identify conditions that causes energy waste and suggest actions to reduce waste
- Interview customers to obtain data related to household energy use such as type of heating system, number of persons at home during day, furnace temperature setting and prior heating costs
- Draw sketch of house, measures house perimeter, windows, and doors using tape measure and record dimensions on sketch for use in heat-loss calculations
- Inspect areas of house such as attics, crawl spaces, basements, and note conditions that contribute to energy waste such as loose-fitting of windows, uninsulated pipes and deficient insulation
- Read hot water tank label to ascertain tank heat-loss rating and determine need for tank insulation blanket
- Examine furnace air filters and heat exchanger to detect dirt in filters and soot built up in exchanger that retards efficient furnace operation
- Confer with customer and recommends action to be taken to reduce energy waste such as weather stripping, reducing hot water temperature setting and adding insulation
- Inform customer about types and prices of energy efficiency items sold by utility
- Conduct research studies to develop theories or methods of abating or controlling sources of environmental pollutants
- Determine data collection methods to be employed in research projects and surveys

- Identify and analyse sources of pollution to determine their effects
- Collect and synthesize data derived from pollution emission measurements, atmospheric monitoring, meteorological and mineralogical information and soil or water samples

Scope

- Forest department
- Urban development
- Industries
- Water resources and agriculture
- Distilleries
- Fertilizer plants
- Water treatment industries
- Refineries
- Textile mills
- Mines and food processing industries

Engineering Physics
Area of work

- Conduct research into phases of physical phenomena, develop theories and laws on the basis of observation and experiments, and devise methods to apply laws and theories of physics to industry, medicine and other fields
- Perform experiments with masers, lasers, cyclotrons, betatrons, telescopes, mass spectrometers, electron microscopes and other equipment to observe structure and properties of matter, transformation and propagation of energy, relationships between matter and energy and other physical phenomena
- Describe observations and conclusions in mathematical terms
- Devise procedures for physical testing of materials
- Conduct instrumental analysis to determine physical properties of materials

Scope

- Space science
- Superconductivity
- Optical materials
- Nuclear engineering

- Nano and micro device engineering
- Photonics
- Positions in Research and Development at high-technology industries
- National laboratories and universities
- Staff engineer
- Scientist
- Technical director

Environmental Engineering and Management
Area of work

- Collection, transport, processing or disposal, managing, monitoring of solid waste materials
- Environmental impact assessment and mitigation
- Water supply and treatment
- Waste heat conveyance

Scope

- Urban development
- Industries
- Water resources and agriculture
- Distilleries
- Fertilizer plants
- Water treatment industries
- Refineries
- Textile mills
- Mines and food processing industries
- Teacher in any reputed University

Fire Engineering
Area of work

- Devise fire brigade call systems, fire detection systems, active fire protection systems, passive fire protection systems
- Smoke control and management
- Devise escape facilities
- Building design/layout/space management
- Fire prevention programs, fire dynamics and modelling
- Human behaviour analysis during fire events
- Risk analysis

- Wildfire management
- Conduct research to determine cause and methods of preventing fires and prepare educational materials concerning fire prevention
- Advise and assist private and public organizations and military services for purposes of safeguarding life and property against fire, explosion and related hazards
- Design or recommend material or equipment such as structural components protection, fire-detection equipment, alarm systems, fire extinguishing devices and systems, and advice on location, handling, installation and maintenance
- Recommend materials, equipment or methods for alleviation of conditions conducive to fire
- Devise fire protection programs, organize and train personnel to carry out such programs
- Conduct research and tests on fire retardants and fire safety of materials and devices to determine fire causes and methods of fire prevention
- May determine fire causes and methods of fire prevention
- May teach courses on fire prevention and protection at accredited educational institutions
- May advice and plan for prevention of destruction by fire, wind, water or other causes of damage

Scope

- Oil refineries
- Petroleum industry
- Fire safety equipment companies
- Forestry/forest preservation boards
- Electronics companies manufacturing fire alarms

Food Engineering
Area of work

- Research and development of new foods, drugs, biological and pharmaceutical products
- Installation of food, biological, pharmaceutical production processes
- Design and operation of environmentally responsible waste treatment systems

- Apply scientific and engineering principles in research, development, production technology, quality control, packaging, processing and utilization of foods
- Conduct basic research and development of foods
- Develop new and improved methods and systems for food processing, production, quality control, packaging and distribution
- Study methods to improve quality of foods such as flavour, colour, texture, nutritional value, convenience, or physical, chemical, and microbiological composition of foods
- Develop food standards, safety and sanitary regulations, and waste management and water supply specifications
- Test new products in test kitchen and develop specific processing methods in laboratory pilot plant, and confer with process engineers, flavour experts, and packaging and marketing specialists to resolve problems
- May specialize in one phase of food technology such as product development, quality control, or production inspection, technical writing, teaching, or consulting
- May specialize in particular branch of food technology, such as cereal grains, meat and poultry, fats and oils, seafood, animal foods, beverages, dairy products, flavours, sugars and starches, stabilizers, preservatives, colours, and nutritional additives, and be identified according to branch of food technology

Scope

- Food packaging industry
- Packaged food analyst
- Government surveyor and auditor
- R&D for food processing units

Forensic Engineering
Area of work

- Investigation of materials, products, components that fail or do not operate or function as intended causing personal injury and damage to property
- Investigation to locate cause or causes of failure to improve performance or life of components
- Assist in court to determine the facts of an accident

- Use scientific methods to determine the cause of an incident and the steps involved
- Basic job duties are to determine what happened in an incident, prepare a findings report and, if required, testify in court
- Forensic engineer also needs to understand the legal practices involved in testifying in court, including the standards of proof writing, speaking and evidence-handling

Scope

- Legal investigator
- Crime/mishap analyser
- Government advisor

Genetic Engineering
Area of work

- Use the techniques of molecular cloning and transformation to alter the structure and characteristics of genes directly
- Genetic engineering has applications in medicine, research, industry and agriculture and can be used on a wide range of plants, animals and micro-organism
- Conduct research along with life scientists, chemists, and medical scientists, on the engineering aspects of the biological systems of humans and animals
- Design and deliver technology to assist people with disabilities
- Keep documentation of service histories on all biomedical equipment
- Advise and assist in the application of instrumentation in clinical environments
- Conduct training to educate clinicians and other personnel on proper use of equipment
- Design and develop medical diagnostic and clinical instrumentation, equipments and procedures using the principles of engineering and bio-behavioural sciences
- Develop new applications for energy sources such as using nuclear power for bio-medical implants
- Evaluate the safety, efficiency and effectiveness of bio-medical equipment
- Analyse new medical procedures to forecast likely outcomes
- Install, adjust, maintain, repair or provide technical support for biomedical equipment

- Write documents describing protocols, policies, standards for use, maintenance and repair of medical equipment
- Research new materials to be used for products such as implanted artificial organs

Scope

- Hospitals
- Research institutes
- Gene scientist
- University professor

Geo-technical and Geo-environmental Engineering
Area of work

- Address environmental problems such as waste disposal and soil improvement
- Involve geo-technical engineering methods which deal with the study, design and construction of earth and earth-supported structures
- Cover the mechanics, dynamics and behaviour of soil, waste management and containment
- Field investigation includes gathering data, implementing lab tests and investigating computer-generated analysis
- Office duties are writing and preparing project proposals, writing lab results, calculating analytical findings and using computer programs for two and three dimensional simulated experiments
- Deal with the analysis, design and construction of earth and earth supported structures to the application of environmental problems such as waste containment, waste disposal and construction of landfills, soil permeation and soil analysis and soil improvement
- Include instruction in soil mechanics, soil dynamics, soil behaviour, waste management and containment systems, geo-synthetics, geo-chemistry, earth structures, geo-environmental engineering, geo-technical engineering, earthquake engineering and foundation engineering

Scope

- Project managers for companies
- Civil engineer associates

- Geological analyst
- Government based structure surveyor
- Drilling companies
- Oil refineries

Hydraulic Engineering
Area of work

- Concerned with the flow and conveyance of fluids, principally water and sewage
- Application of fluid mechanics principles to problems dealing with the collection, storage, control, transport, regulation, measurement and use of water
- Design and direct construction of power and other hydraulic engineering projects for control and use of water
- Compute and estimate rates of water flow
- Specify type and size of equipment such as conduits, pumps, turbines, pressure valves and surge tanks used in transporting water and converting water power into electricity
- Direct the activities of workers engaged in dredging, digging cut offs, placing jetties and constructing levees to stabilize streams or open water ways
- Design and coordinate construction of artificial canals, conduits and mains to transport and distribute water
- Plan reservoirs, pressure valves and booster stations to obtain proper water pressure at all levels

Scope

- Marine industry
- Airlines and shipping industry
- Oil/gas pipeline companies
- Automobile industry
- Home appliances manufacturers

Industrial Engineering
Area of work

- Apply statistical methods and perform mathematical calculations to determine manufacturing processes, staff requirements and production standards

- Coordinate quality control objectives and activities to resolve production problems, maximize product reliability and minimize cost
- Confer with vendors, staff and management personnel regarding purchases, procedures, product specifications, manufacturing capabilities and project status
- Draft and design layout of equipment, materials and workspace to illustrate maximum efficiency, using drafting tools and computer
- Review production schedules, engineering specifications, orders and related information to obtain knowledge of manufacturing methods, procedures and activities
- Communicate with management and user personnel to develop production and design standards
- Study functional statements, organization charts and project information to determine functions and responsibilities of workers and work units
- Establish work measurement programs and analyse work samples to develop standards for labour utilization
- Analyse work force utilization, facility layout and operational data such as production costs, process flow charts and production schedules to determine efficient utilization of workers and equipment
- Recommend methods for improving worker efficiency and reducing waste of materials and utilities such as restructuring job duties, reorganizing work flow, relocating work stations and equipment and purchase of equipment
- Confer with management and engineering staff to implement plans and recommendations
- May develop management systems for cost analysis, financial planning, wage and salary administration and job evaluation
- Plan utilization of facilities, equipment, materials and personnel to improve efficiency of operations

Scope

- Amusement parks
- Dockyard and shipping industry
- Automobile industry
- Appliances companies
- Construction firms
- Metal manufacturers

- Production analysts
- University Professors
- Government auditors
- Transportation industry

Industrial Tribology and Maintenance Engineering
Area of work

- Include the study and application of the principles of friction, lubrication and wear
- Analyse engineering design of proposed product such as aircraft, naval vessel, or electronic control or navigation system, and submit specifications for maintenance requirements
- Analyse customer's initial proposal for product utilization and recommend basic product specifications and techniques for satisfying customer requirements
- Review engineering specifications and drawings during development and proposes design refinements to improve ratio of operational time to maintenance time
- Participate in engineering discussions concerning design alternatives effecting product maintainability
- Determine crew makeup, training requirements and maintenance time by evaluating data from tests and maintainability programs of related products
- Review subcontractor technical practices for assuring maintainability of equipment and parts and submit evaluation for management decision
- Specify standardized tests or draft new test programs for demonstrating product maintainability in company or supplier test
- Observe maintainability tests at supplier and plant locations to verify operations are conducted according to standards

Scope

- Manufacturing industry
- Plant maintenance supervisor
- Government auditor/analyst
- Automobile companies
- Oil/gas/coal industry
- Official government consultants

Instrument Engineering
Area of work

- Focus on the principle and operation of measuring instruments that are used in design and configuration of automated systems in electrical, pneumatic domains etc
- Typically work for industries with automated processes such as chemical or manufacturing plants with the goal of improving system productivity, reliability, safety, optimization and stability
- Responsible for integrating the sensors with the recorders, transmitters, displays or control systems
- May design or specify installation, wiring and signal conditioning
- May be responsible for calibration, testing and maintenance of the system
- Responsible for designing, developing, installing, managing and/ or maintaining equipment which is used to monitor and control engineering systems, machinery and processes

Scope

- Environment agencies
- Nuclear power industry
- Thermal power industry
- Government sector of power
- Weapons manufacturers
- Accurate systems manufacturers
- Precise calculation instruments manufacturers

Integrated Electronics and Circuits
Area of work

- Designing of ICs (An integrated circuit or monolithic integrated circuit is a set of electronic circuits on one small plate of semiconductor material, normally silicon)
- Perform any combination of tasks to fabricate integrated circuits on semiconductor wafers according to written specifications
- Load semiconductor wafers into processing containers for processing or into inspection equipment using tweezers or vacuum wand
- Clean and dry photo masks and semiconductor wafers to remove contaminants using cleaning and drying equipment

- Inspect photo masks and wafers for defects such as scratches using microscope, magnifying lens or computer-aided inspection equipment
- Deposit layer of photoresist solution on wafers using automated equipment
- Align photo mask pattern on photoresist layer, expose pattern to ultraviolet light and develop pattern using specialized equipment
- Alter electrical nature of wafer layers according to photo mask patterns to form integrated circuits on wafers, using equipment, such as acid baths, diffusion furnaces, ion implant equipment, and metallization equipment
- Remove photoresist from wafers using stripping chemicals and equipment
- Inspect and measure circuitry for conformance to pattern specifications using microscope with measuring attachment
- Test functioning of circuitry, using electronic test equipment and standard procedures

Scope

- Appliances industries (home and defence)
- Jobs in defence sector
- Specialized circuit fabricators in companies
- Fire alarm manufacturers
- Computer devices manufacturing firms
- Weapon industry
- Almost in every electronics industry

Material Science and Engineering
Area of work

- Understand microstructure of solids
- Understand materials processes and apply general natural science and engineering principles to the analysis and design of materials systems
- Concerned with the design, fabrication and optimal selection of engineering materials that must simultaneously fulfil dimensional, property, quality control and economic requirements
- Evaluate technical and economic factors, recommending engineering and manufacturing actions for attainment of design objectives of process or product

- Review plans for new product and factors such as strength, weight and cost to submit material selection recommendations ensuring attainment of design objectives
- Plan and implement laboratory operations to develop material and fabrication procedures for new materials to fulfil product cost and performance standards
- Confer with producers of materials such as metals, ceramics or polymers during investigation and evaluation of materials suitable for specific product applications
- Review product failure data and interpret laboratory tests and analyse to establish or rule out material and process causes
- Conduct scientific studies for understanding, characterizing and developing materials leading to potential uses for the benefit of science and emerging technologies
- Conduct programs for studying structures and properties of various materials such as metals, alloys, ceramics, semiconductors and polymers to obtain research data
- Plan experimental laboratory production of materials having special characteristics to confirm feasibility of processes and techniques for potential users
- Prepare reports of materials studies for information of other scientists and requestors
- May guide technical staff engaged in developing materials for specific use in projected product or device

Scope

- Polymer industry
- Textile industry
- Construction agencies
- University professor
- Plastic goods manufacturers
- Research and development of new materials

Mechanical Engineering
Area of work

- Research and Development
- Draft technical drawings, manually or with the aid of computers
- Supervise the manufacturing of mechanical components and machines

- Analyse and test different types of machines and their parts to ensure that they function flawlessly
- Install machines and mechanical parts at the client location
- Ensure that machinery is working as per specifications
- Research, plan and design mechanical and electro-mechanical products and systems
- Direct and coordinate activities involved in fabrication, operation, application, installation and repair of mechanical or electromechanical products and systems
- Research and analyse data such as customer design proposal, specifications and manuals to determine feasibility of design or application
- Design products or systems such as instruments, controls, robots, engines, machines, and mechanical, thermal, hydraulic, or heat transfer systems
- Direct and coordinate fabrication and installation activities to ensure products and systems conform to engineering design and customer specifications
- Coordinate operation, maintenance and repair activities to obtain optimum utilization of machines and equipment

Scope

- Automobile industry
- Sheet metal fabrication companies
- Metallurgical processes companies
- Defence services
- Transportation
- Medical industry
- Agricultural industry
- Aerospace industry
- Automotive industry
- Heating and cooling systems manufacturers

Mining Engineering
Area of work

- Involve the practice, science, the theory, the technology and application of extracting and processing minerals from a naturally occurring environment
- Include processing minerals for additional uses

- Concerned with mitigation of damage to the environment as a result of that production and processing

Scope

- Steel authority of India
- Oil and Natural Gas Corporation
- Mine research organisation
- Management and consultation agencies of mined resources

Molecular Engineering
Area of work

- Manufacturing molecules
- Seems to converge with mechanical engineering, since the molecules being designed often resemble small machines
- Used to create new molecules which may not exist in nature on an extremely small scale
- Precision form of chemical engineering that includes protein engineering, the creation of protein molecules, a process that occurs naturally in biochemistry
- Important part of pharmaceutical research and materials science
- Sometimes called Nanotechnology

Scope

- Nano-medicine
- Bio-informatics
- Stem cell development research companies
- Pharmaceutical companies
- Space research
- Academics
- Nano-toxicology
- Electronics/semiconductor industry
- Materials science including textiles, polymers, packaging etc
- Auto and aerospace industries
- Sporting goods
- Medical fields and pharmaceuticals
- Environmental monitoring, control, and remediation
- Food science including quality control and packaging
- Forensics

Naval Architecture and Offshore Engineering
Area of work

- Combine two main areas related to sea namely naval architecture and offshore engineering
- Specialization in:

  o naval architecture
  o hydrodynamics
  o ship transportation
  o project management
  o marine engineering systems
  o structure design
  o production technology

Scope

- Government and private shipyards
- Ship design offices
- Boatyards
- Classification societies
- Offshore companies
- Marine/offshore engineering companies
- Shipbuilding
- Power generation ship systems
- Naval architecture

Neural Engineering
Area of work

- Understand, repair and replace or enhance neural systems
- Solve design problems of living neural tissues and non-living constructs
- Combined with robotics to perform automation tasks at the neural level
- Aim to treat disease or injury by employing medical device technologies that would enhance or suppress activity of the nervous system with the delivery of pharmaceutical agents, electrical signals, or other forms of energy stimulus to re-establish balance in impaired regions of the brain or simply neuro-modulation

- Apply neuro-science and engineering to investigate peripheral and central nervous system function and to find clinical solutions to problems created by brain damage or malfunction

Scope

- Neural imaging expert and consultant
- Neural networks (computer science industry)
- Companies manufacturing brain computer interfaces
- Microsystems industry
- Neuro-robotics industry

Optical Engineering
Area of work

- Field of study that focuses on applications of optics
- Design components of optical instruments such as lenses, microscopes, telescopes and other equipment that utilize the properties of light
- Design optical systems with specific characteristics to fit within specified physical limits of precision optical instruments such as still- and motion-picture cameras, lens systems, telescopes and viewing and display devices
- Determine specifications for operations and makes adjustments to calibrate and obtain specified operational performance
- Design mounts for components to hold them in proper planes in relation to each other and instrument in which they will be used
- Design inspection instruments to test optical systems for defects such as aberrations and deviations

Scope

- Research and development (optics and devices industry)
- Electronics industry
- Home appliances manufacturers
- Optical components and systems manufacturers
- Communication industry
- Space research
- Scientist (optical science)

Opto-Electronics and Optical Communication
Area of work

- Study and application of electronic devices that detect and control the light
- Design devices like electrical-to-optical or optical-to-electrical transducers, or instruments that use such devices in their operation

Scope

- Research and development (optics and devices industry)
- Electronics industry
- Home appliances manufacturers
- Optical components and systems manufacturers
- Communication industry
- Space research
- Scientist (optical science)

Petroleum Engineering
Area of work

- Analyse technical and cost factors to plan methods to recover maximum oil and gas in oil-field operations
- Examine map of subsurface oil and gas reservoir locations to recommend placement of wells to maximize economical production from reservoir
- Evaluate probable well production rate during natural or stimulated-flow production phases
- Recommend supplementary processes to enhance recovery involving stimulation of flow by use of processes such as pressurizing or heating in subsurface regions
- Analyse recommendations of reservoir engineering specialist for placement of well in oil field
- Develop well drilling plan for management approval, specifying factors including drilling time, number of special operations, such as directional drilling, and testing, and material requirements and costs including well casing and drilling muds
- Provide technical consultation during drilling operations to resolve problems such as bore directional change, unsatisfactory drilling rate or invasion of subsurface water in well bore

- Advise substitution of drilling mud compounds or tool bits to improve drilling conditions
- Inspect well to determine that final casing and tubing installations are completed
- Plan oil and gas field recovery containers, piping, and treatment vessels to receive, remove contaminants, and separate oil and gas products flowing from well
- Monitor production rate of gas or oil from established wells and plans rework process to correct well production, such as repacking of well bore and additional perforation of subsurface sands adjacent to well bottom

Scope

- Petroleum Industry
- Oil refineries
- Investor Consultant
- Drilling Engineers
- Oil Rig managers

Polymer Science and Technology
Area of work

- Subfield of materials science concerned with polymers, primarily synthetic polymers such as plastics
- Includes researchers in multiple disciplines including chemistry, physics and engineering
- Can work in any of the following disciplines: Polymer chemistry or macromolecular chemistry, Polymer physics, Polymer characterization etc

Scope

- Polymer Manufacturer
- Chemicals manufacturer
- Paint industry
- Rubber Industry
- Tyre Industry
- Plastic manufacturer
- Adhesive Manufacturer
- Fibre synthesising industry

Power System Engineering
Area of work

- Involve high voltage DC transmissions, power system dynamics and control, power system transients and protection, power system analysis and operation and power system transmission systems
- Lay out plans and estimate costs for constructing transmission lines
- Visit proposed construction site and select best and shortest route to avoid interference with telephone or other lines
- Submit data on proposed route to right-of-way department for obtaining necessary easements
- Arrange for aerial, topographical, and other surveys to be made to obtain pertinent data for planning lines
- Devise steel and wood supporting structures for cables and draws sketch showing their location
- Perform detailed engineering calculations to draw up construction specifications such as cable sag, pole strength and necessary grounding
- Estimate labour, material, and construction costs, and draws up specifications for purchase of materials and equipment
- Keep informed on new developments in electric power transmission
- Assist various departments of Power Company on problems involving transmission-line operation and maintenance
- Inspect completed installation

Scope

- Grade 2 Technician
- Junior Engineer at power plants
- Steel and chemical plants
- Public sector and private sector: electricity boards, large scale industries, manufacturing plants etc
- Natural gas plants
- Research projects
- Thermal and nuclear corporations
- Job opportunities in different industries like telecommunication, marketing, power transmission, power generation, electrical, electronics

Production and Industrial Engineering
Area of work

- Designing and developing a device, assembly or system such that it is produced as an item for sale through some production manufacturing process
- Deal with issues of cost, producibility, quality, performance, reliability, serviceability and user features
- Develop the concept of the product, and the design and development of its mechanical, electronics and software components
- Plan and coordinate production procedures in industrial plant
- Direct production departments
- Regulate and coordinate functions of office and shop
- Introduce efficient production line methods
- Initiate and direct procedures to increase company output

Scope

- Public and private sector
- Manufacturing organizations
- Information and control systems
- Computer controlled inspection
- Assembly and handling
- Hospitals
- Agriculture manufacturing

Production Engineering
Area of work

- Combination of manufacturing technology with management science
- To accomplish the production process in the smoothest, most-judicious and most economical way
- Application of castings, machining, processing, joining processes, metal cutting & tool design, metrology, machine tools, machining systems, automation, jigs and fixtures, and die and mould design and material science and design of automobile parts and machine designing and manufacturing
- Production engineering overlap substantially with manufacturing engineering and industrial engineering

Scope

- Public and private sector
- Manufacturing organizations
- Information and control systems
- Computer controlled inspection
- Assembly and handling
- Hospitals
- Agriculture manufacturing

Railway System Engineering
Area of work

- Deal with design, construction and operation of all types of railway systems
- Design railroad and street railway tracks, terminals, yards, and other facilities and directs and coordinates construction and relocation of facilities
- Plan roadbed, rail size, and curves to meet train speed and load requirements
- Direct construction of bridges, culverts, buildings and other structures
- Direct track and roadway maintenance
- Survey traffic problems related to street railway system and recommend grade revisions, additional trackage, use of heavier power, and other changes to relieve congestion and reduce hazards

Scope

- Railway industry
- Government inspection/auditing agencies

Rehabilitation Engineering
Area of work

- Systematic application of engineering sciences to design, develop, adapt, test, evaluate, apply, and distribute technological solutions to problems fronted by individuals with disabilities
- Functional areas addressed through rehabilitation engineering may include mobility, communications, hearing, vision, and cognition, and activities associated with employment,

independent living, education, and integration into the community

Scope

- Government rehabilitation agencies
- Social worker
- Project planner (rehab)
- Other public sector agencies

Robotics Engineering
Area of work

- Deal with the design, construction, operation, structural disposition, manufacture and application of robots
- Related to science of electronics, engineering, mechanics and software

Scope

- Commerce retail services fields
- Power plants
- Manufacturing
- Research
- Agriculture
- R&D robotics
- Military programs
- Space programs
- Transportation
- Warehouses
- Hospitals

Safety Engineering
Area of work

- Attempt to reduce the frequency of failures, and ensure that when failures do occur, the consequences are not life threatening
- Anticipate, identify and evaluate hazardous conditions and practices
- Develop hazard control designs, methods, procedures and programs

- Implement, administer and advise others on hazard control programs
- Measure, audit and evaluate the effectiveness of hazard control programs
- Draft a future safety plan and statement based on real time experiences and facts

Scope

- Manufacturing industry
- Hazard coping government agencies
- Safety equipment manufacturers
- Disaster management teams
- Legal reviewer
- Legal auditor for court and other legal purposes
- Insurance companies

Space Technology
Area of work

- Technology related to entering and retrieving objects or life forms from space
- Technologies such as weather forecasting, remote sensing, GPS systems, satellite television, long distance communication can benefit from space technology

Scope

- ISRO-Indian space research org
- DRDO-defence research and development org
- HAL-Hindustan aeronautics limited
- NAL-national aeronautical laboratory
- NASA

Structural Engineering
Area of work

- Direct or participate in planning, designing, or reviewing plans for erection of structures requiring stress analysis
- Design structure to meet estimated load requirements, computing size, shape, strength, and type of structural members,

or performs structural analysis of plans and structures prepared by private engineers
- Design of buildings and large non-building structures
- Design of machinery
- Design of medical equipment
- Design of vehicles

Scope

- Structural inspectors
- Housing and building industry
- Automobile manufacturing
- Defence services
- Space craft manufacturing
- Aid to civil and architecture industry
- Ship building industry

System Engineering
Area of work

- Deal with work processes, optimisation methods, risk management tools
- Overlap human-centred disciplines such as control engineering, industrial engineering, organizational studies, project management etc
- Analyse user requirements, procedures, and problems to automate processing or to improve existing computer system
- Confer with personnel of organizational units involved to analyse current operational procedures, identify problems, and learn specific input and output requirements, such as forms of data input, how data is to be summarized, and formats for reports
- Write detailed description of user needs, program functions, and steps required to develop or modify computer program
- Review computer system capabilities, workflow, and scheduling limitations to determine if requested program or program change is possible within existing system
- Study existing information processing systems to evaluate effectiveness and develop new systems to improve production or workflow as required

- Prepare workflow charts and diagrams to specify in detail operations to be performed by equipment and computer programs and operations to be performed by personnel in system
- Conduct studies pertaining to development of new information systems to meet current and projected needs
- Plan and prepare technical reports, memoranda, and instructional manuals as documentation of program development
- Upgrade system and correct errors to maintain system after implementation
- May assist computer programmers in resolution of work problems related to flow charts, project specifications, or programming
- May prepare time and cost estimates for completing projects

Scope

- Electronics Companies
- Integrated System Manufacturers
- IT Industry
- High End Computer System Manufacturers
- Real Time System Manufacturers
- Testing Departments

Tele-Communication Engineering
Area of work

- The work ranges from basic circuit design to strategic mass developments
- Designing of telecom equipments, electronic switching systems, copper telephone facilities, fibre optics and their installations
- Overlap with broadcast engineering

Scope

- Jobs in Tele-communication Companies
- Civil, Telecom and Power Departments
- Power Sector
- Defence Services
- Space Organisations
- Signal Processing Agencies
- Electronic Equipment Manufacturers

Textile Technology
Area of work

- Concerned with the application of scientific principles and engineering practices to the wide ranging aspects of textile processes, products and machinery including synthetic fibres
- Health and safety
- Pollution control
- Energy management
- Textile technologists work closely with chemical engineers to develop new materials for a variety of purposes like packaging materials that can keep food fresh longer, fire-proof upholstery for vehicles, lighter or warmer fabric for space travel, better bandages for internal and external use

Scope

- Aerospace Industry
- Medicine Industry
- Architecture Field
- Automotive Industry
- Apparel Industry
- Sports Industry

Transportation Engineering
Area of work

- Planning, functional design, operation and management of facilities for any mode of transportation in order to provide for the safe, efficient, rapid, comfortable, convenient, economical and environmentally compatible movement of people and goods
- It is a sub-discipline of civil engineering and of industrial engineering
- Develop plans for surface transportation projects according to established engineering standards and state or federal construction policy
- Prepare plans, estimates and specifications to design transportation facilities
- Plan alterations and modifications of existing streets, highways, and freeways to improve traffic flow
- Prepare deeds, property descriptions and right-of-way maps

- Perform field engineering calculations to compensate for change orders and contract estimates

Scope

- Environmental Legislations
- Transportation Systems
- Traffic Safety
- Traffic Operations
- Highway, Airport, Railway Management
- Transportation device manufacturing
- System engineer

VLSI Design, Tool and Technology
Area of work

- Create integrated circuits
- Emphasize on structure and function of complete system
- Provide necessary expertise required by the industry

Scope

- Jobs in multi-national companies

Water Resource Engineering
Area of work

- Supply water for human use
- Remove water when humans are finished using it
- Develop methods of avoiding damage from excess water
- Planning and management of constructed facilities that address the above tasks
- Planning, development and managing of water resources
- Design, build and manage water intakes, water treatment plants and the network of pipes that convey water to homes and industrial requirements
- May be involved in design, construction or maintenance of rain water harvesting and re-use systems, dams, pipelines, pumping stations, locks and seaport facilities
- Work to prevent floods, to supply water for cities, industry and irrigation to treat waste water, to protect beaches, to manage and reuse rain water, to institute water sensitive urban design

Scope

- Government authorities
- Climate change impact planning
- Hydrologist
- Designing and engineering of water systems

Welding Engineering
Area of work

- Develop welding techniques and procedures
- Application of welding equipment to problems involving fabrication of metals
- Conduct research and development investigations to develop and test new fabrication processes and procedures, improve existing or develop new welding equipment
- Develop new or modify current welding methods, techniques, and procedures, discover new patterns of welding phenomena, or to correlate and substantiate hypotheses
- Prepare technical reports as result of research and development
- Preventive maintenance investigations
- Establish welding procedures to guide production and welding personnel relating to specification restrictions, material processes, pre- and post-heating requirements which involve use of complex alloys, unusual fabrication methods, welding of critical joints, and complex post heating requirements
- Evaluate new developments in welding field for possible application to current welding problems or production processes
- Direct and coordinate technical personnel in performing inspections to ensure workers' compliance with established welding procedures, restrictions, and standards
- In testing welds for conformance with national code requirements or testing welding personnel for certification
- Contact personnel of other agencies, engineering personnel, or clients to exchange ideas, information, or offer technical advice concerning welding matters
- May perform experimental welding to evaluate new equipment, techniques, and materials

Scope

- Manufacturing engineer

- Automotive production consultant
- Manufacturing consultant
- Construction supervisor
- Welding engineer
- Weld shop supervisor

Medical Careers

The other option available for students choosing science stream is Medical Careers. This stream also offers innumerable career options and opportunities to students.

The minimum qualification required for medical is XII or equivalent with good marks having subjects Physics, Chemistry and Biology.

There are many colleges, institutions and universities offering medical courses to students. Many of these give admission based on ranking in entrance test and also need a minimum qualification. On the other side, many of these are giving admissions to students without taking any entrance test. Some of the choices available for students opting for medical career are:

Addiction Medicine
Area of work

- Deal with the prevention and treatment of addictive disease
- Work in other areas like public health, psychology, social work, mental health counselling, psychiatry and internal medicine
- Physicians specializing in this field are in general agreement concerning applicability of treatment to those with addiction to drugs

Scope

- Clinics, Hospitals, Universities and Private consultation

Allergy and Immunology
Area of work

- Evaluation, diagnosis and management of disorders involving the immune system
- The allergist/immunologist is trained in:

- o Allergy testing
- o History-allergy test correlation
- o Bronchoprovocation testing
- o Environmental control instructions
- o Inhalant immunotherapy
- o Immunomodulation therapy
- o Venom immunotherapy
- o Food and drug challenges
- o Drug desensitization
- o Evaluation of immune competence
- o Education

Scope

- Clinics, Hospitals, Universities and Private consultation

Anaesthesiology
Area of work

- Provide pain relief and maintenance or restoration of a stable condition during and immediately following an operation or an obstetric or diagnostic procedure
- Assess the risk of the patient undergoing surgery and optimize the patient's condition prior to, during and after surgery
- Provide medical management and consultation in pain management and critical care medicine
- Diagnose and treat acute, long-standing and cancer pain problems, critical illnesses and severe injuries
- Direct resuscitation in the care of patients with cardiac or respiratory emergencies, including the need for artificial ventilation as well as supervise post anaesthesia recovery
- Anaesthesiologists can work in the following subspecialties:

  - o Critical care medicine, which involves diagnosing, treating, and supporting critically ill and injured patients, particularly trauma victims and patients with multiple organ dysfunctions
  - o Hospice and palliative medicine, which involves preventing and relieving the suffering experienced by patients with life-limiting illnesses
  - o Pain medicine, which involves diagnosing and treating of the entire range of painful disorders

- Care for patients experiencing problems with acute, chronic and cancer pain

Scope

- Clinics, Hospitals, Universities and Private consultation

Audiology
Area of work

- An audiologist is a health-care professional specializing in identifying, diagnosing, treating and monitoring disorders of the auditory and vestibular system portions of the ear
- Audiologists are trained to diagnose, manage and treat hearing or balance problems
- Dispense hearing aids
- Recommend and map cochlear implants

Scope

- Clinics, Hospitals, Universities and Private consultation

Bachelor of Ayurveda, Medicine and Surgery (BAMS)
Area of work

- Bachelor of Ayurveda, Medicine and Surgery (B.A.M.S.) is a medical degree in India and is the study of traditional Ayurvedic system of treatment of diseases

Scope

- Clinics, Hospitals, Universities and Private consultation

Bariatrician
Area of work

- Weight loss doctor specialized in the treatment of obesity and its associated conditions without surgical intervention
- Help prevent obesity related diseases by reducing body fat responsible for the disease processes while maintaining muscle mass
- There are bariatric surgeons also who perform weight-loss surgeries

Scope

- Clinics, Hospitals, Universities and Private consultation

Bachelor of Homoeopathic Medicine and Surgery (BHMS)
Area of work

- Bachelor of Homoeopathic Medicine and Surgery (B.H.M.S.) is a medical degree in India and is the study of traditional homoeopathic system of treatment of diseases

Scope

- Clinics, Hospitals, Universities and Private consultation

Cardiac Electrophysiology
Area of work

- Diagnosing and treating the electrical activities of the heart
- A specialist in cardiac electrophysiology is known as a cardiac electrophysiologist

Scope

- Clinics, Hospitals, Universities and Private consultation

Chiropractic
Area of work

- Diagnosis, treatment and prevention of disorders of the neuromusculoskeletal system including but not limited to back pain, neck pain, pain in the joints of the arms or legs, and headaches
- Doctors practising this are often referred as chiropractors or chiropractic physicians
- Chiropractors have broad diagnostic skills and are also trained to recommend therapeutic and rehabilitative exercises, as well as to provide nutritional, dietary and lifestyle counselling

Scope

- Clinics, Hospitals, Universities and Private consultation

Colon and Rectal Surgery
Area of work

- Diagnose and treat various diseases of the small intestine, colon, rectum, anal canal and perianal area by medical and surgical means
- Deals with other organs and tissues (such as the liver, urinary and female reproductive system) involved with primary intestinal disease
- Have the expertise to diagnose and manage anorectal conditions such as hemorrhoids, fissures, abscesses, and fistulas
- They also treat problems of the intestine and colon and perform endoscopic procedures to evaluate and treat problems such as cancer, polyps (precancerous growths) and inflammatory conditions

Scope

- Clinics, Hospitals, Universities and Private consultation

Cytopathology
Area of work

- A branch of pathology that studies and diagnoses diseases on the cellular level
- Used to investigate thyroid lesions, diseases involving sterile body cavities (peritoneal, pleural, and cerebrospinal) and a wide range of other body sites
- Used to aid in the diagnosis of cancer
- Helps in the diagnosis of certain infectious diseases and other inflammatory conditions

Scope

- Clinics, Hospitals, Universities and Private consultation

Dentistry
Area of work

- Diagnosis, prevention and treatment of diseases and conditions of the oral cavity

- Carry out dental treatments such as restorative (dental restorations, crowns, and bridges), orthodontics (braces), prosthetic (dentures), endodontic (root canal) therapy, periodontal (gum) therapy and exodontia (extraction of teeth)
- Various persons working in dentistry and related fields are Dental Assistant, Dental Hygienist, Paediatric Dentist, and Dental Laboratory Technician

Scope

- Clinics, Hospitals, Universities and Private consultation

Dermatology
Area of work

- Diagnose and treat paediatric and adult patients with disorders of the skin, mouth, external genitalia, hair and nails as well as a number of sexually transmitted diseases
- Can get expertise in the management of cosmetic disorders of the skin such as hair loss, scars and the skin changes associated with aging
- Dermatologists can receive training in the following subspecialties:

  o Dermatopathology, which involves diagnosing and monitoring diseases of the skin including infectious, immunologic, degenerative and neoplastic diseases
  o Paediatric dermatology, which involves treating specific skin disease categories with emphasis on those diseases which predominate in infants, children and adolescents
  o Procedural dermatology, which involves studying, diagnosing and surgical treating of diseases of the skin and adjacent mucous membranes, cutaneous appendages, hair, nails and subcutaneous tissue

Scope

- Clinics, Hospitals, Universities and Private consultation

Dieticians and Nutritionists
Area of work

- Guide you regarding your diet, either for overcoming weight problem or as a complimentary therapy with your main treatment for overcoming diseases

Scope

- Clinics, Hospitals, Universities and Private consultation

Emergency Medicine
Area of work

- Focus on the immediate decision making and action necessary to prevent death or any further disability both in the pre-hospital setting by directing emergency medical technicians as well as in the emergency department
- The emergency physician provides immediate recognition, evaluation, care, stabilization and disposition of a generally diversified population of adult and paediatric patients in response to acute illness and injury
- Emergency medicine physicians can receive training in these subspecialties:

  o Hospice and palliative medicine, which involves preventing and relieving the suffering experienced by patients with life-limiting illnesses
  o Medical toxicology, which uses special knowledge to evaluate and manage patients with accidental or purposeful poisoning through drugs or toxins
  o Paediatric emergency medicine, which involves managing emergencies in infants and children and requires special qualifications
  o Sports medicine, which involves the prevention, diagnosis, and treatment of injuries sustained in athletic endeavours, undersea and hyperbaric medicine, which involves treating decompression illness and diving accident cases

Scope

Clinics, Hospitals, Universities and Private consultation

Endocrinology
Area of work

- Study of the biosynthesis, storage, chemistry, biochemical and physiological function of hormones and with the cells of the endocrine glands and tissues that secrete them
- Deal with the coordination of metabolism, respiration, excretion, movement, reproduction and sensory perception depend on chemical cues, substances synthesized and secreted by specialized cells
- An endocrinologist is a physician who specializes in treating disorders of the endocrine system, such as diabetes, hyperthyroidism

Scope

Clinics, Hospitals, Universities and Private consultation

Family Medicine
Area of work

- Concerned with the total health care of the individual and the family
- Diagnose and treat a wide variety of ailments in patients of all ages
- Care for children as well as adults, including the unique needs of women and the elderly
- Family physicians can receive training in the following subspecialties:

  o Adolescent medicine, which requires multidisciplinary training in the unique physical, psychological, and social characteristics of adolescents and their health-care problems and needs
  o Geriatric medicine, which requires knowledge of the aging process including the diagnostic, therapeutic, preventive, and rehabilitative aspects of illness in the elderly
  o Hospice and palliative medicine, which involves preventing and relieving the suffering experienced by patients with life-limiting illnesses
  o Sleep medicine, which involves diagnosing and managing the clinical conditions that occur during sleep, disturb

sleep, or are affected by disturbances

- o Sports medicine, which involves training physicians to be responsible for continuous care related to the enhancement of health and fitness as well as the prevention of injury and illness

Scope

Clinics, Hospitals, Universities and Private consultation

Gastroenterology
Area of work

- Focus on the digestive system and its disorders
- Diseases affecting the gastrointestinal tract, which includes the organs from mouth to anus, along the alimentary canal, are the focus of this specialty

Scope

- Clinics, Hospitals, Universities and Private consultation

General Surgery
Area of work

- Diagnosis and care of patients with diseases and disorders affecting the abdomen, digestive tract, endocrine system, breast, skin and blood vessels
- Trained in the care of paediatric and cancer patients and in the treatment of patients who are injured or critically ill
- Common problems treated by general surgeons include hernias, breast tumours, gallstones, appendicitis, pancreatitis, bowel obstructions, colon inflammation, and colon cancer
- Surgeons can receive training in the following subspecialties:

  - o Hand surgery, which requires expertise in the investigation, preservation, and restoration by medical, surgical, and rehabilitative means, of all structures of the hand and wrist
  - o Hospice and palliative medicine, which involves preventing and relieving the suffering experienced by patients with life-limiting illnesses
  - o Paediatric surgery, which requires expertise in surgical

conditions in premature and new-born infant, children, and adolescents

o Surgical critical care, which requires expertise in the critically ill and postoperative patient, particularly the trauma victim and those with multiple organ dysfunction

o Vascular surgery, which requires expertise in surgical disorders of the blood vessels, excluding the intracranial vessels of the heart

Scope

- Clinics, Hospitals, Universities and Private consultation

Geriatrics
Area of work

- Geriatrics or geriatric medicine is a sub-specialty of internal medicine and family medicine that focuses on health care of elderly people
- Aim to promote health by preventing and treating diseases and disabilities in older adults

Scope

- Clinics, Hospitals, Universities and Private consultation

Health Information Specialist
Area of work

- Analyse finance, insurance, workload data etc
- Help recording the information in a systematic manner and help medical practitioners plan and evaluate the information for their patients
- The health information specialist careers list is as follows:

    o Registered Record Administrators
    o Accredited Record Technicians
    o Certified Medical Billing and Coding Specialist
    o Cancer Registrar
    o Health Information Administrator
    o Medical Coder
    o Medical Librarian

o   Medical Transcriptionist
o   Clinical scientific officers
o   Operating department practitioner

Scope

- Clinics, Hospitals, Universities and Insurance companies

Haematology & Oncology
Area of work

- Diagnosis and treatment of blood diseases, especially blood cell cancers
- This type of doctor is trained in haematology (the study of blood) and oncology (the study of cancer)
- Oncologists should also have some expertise and proficiency in the management of solid tumours
- Some haematologist-oncologists become stem cell transplantation experts

Scope

- Clinics, Hospitals, Universities and Private consultation

Hepatology
Area of work

- Hepatology is the branch of medicine related to the study of liver, gallbladder, biliary tree and pancreas as well as management of their disorders

Scope

- Clinics, Hospitals, Universities and Private consultation

Internal Medicine
Area of work

- Provide long-term comprehensive care managing both common and complex illness of adolescents, adults and the elderly
- Diagnosis and treatment of cancer, infections and other diseases affecting the heart, blood, kidneys and joints

- Diagnosis and treatment of digestive, respiratory and vascular systems
- Understanding of disease prevention, wellness, substance abuse, mental health and effective treatment of common problems of the eyes, ears, skin, nervous system and reproductive organs
- Internists can receive training in the following subspecialties:

  o Adolescent medicine
  o Cardiovascular disease
  o Clinical cardiac electrophysiology
  o Critical care medicine
  o Endocrinology, diabetes & metabolism
  o Gastroenterology
  o Geriatric medicine
  o Haematology
  o Hospice and palliative medicine
  o Infectious disease
  o Interventional cardiology
  o Medical oncology
  o Nephrology
  o Pulmonary disease
  o Rheumatology
  o Sleep medicine
  o Sports medicine
  o Transplant hepatology

Scope

- Clinics, Hospitals, Universities and Private consultation

Laboratory Technician
Area of work

- Identify, diagnose and find the possible line of treatment
- Work with complex lab equipment and procedures
- Doctors rely on their reports for treating the patients
- The careers under this field are:

  o Blood bank technology specialist
  o Clinical Assistant
  o Clinical Laboratory Scientist/Medical Technologist
  o Clinical Laboratory Technician

69

- o Cytogenetic Technologist
- o Cytotechnologist
- o Diagnostic Molecular Scientist
- o Histotechnician
- o Histotechnologist
- o Pathologists
- o Forensic Pathologists
- o Phlebotomist
- o Anatomical pathologist
- o Embryologist

Scope

- Clinics, Hospitals, Universities and Private consultation

Medical Genetics
Area of work

- Diagnostic and therapeutic procedures for patients with genetically-linked diseases
- Plan and coordinate large-scale screening programs for inborn errors of metabolism, hemoglobinopathies, chromosome abnormalities and neural tube defects
- Medical geneticists can receive training in the following subspecialties:
  - o Medical biochemical genetics, which entails the diagnosis and medical management of individuals with inborn errors of metabolism
  - o Molecular genetic pathology, which requires expertise in the principles, theory, and technologies of molecular biology and molecular genetics

Scope

- Clinics, Hospitals, Universities and Private consultation

Medical Imaging
Area of work

- Take and examine images of internal organs, cancerous image, fetus etc

- There are medical imaging technicians who specialize in taking images of heart, brain, pelvis etc
- The following are some of the medical imaging careers list:
    o Diagnostic Medical Sonographer
    o MRI Technician
    o Medical Dosimetrist
    o Nuclear Medicine Technologist
    o Radiation Therapist
    o Radiographer
    o Radiologic Technologist
    o Registered Radiologist Assistant
    o Cardiographer

Scope

- Clinics, Hospitals, Universities and Private consultation

Neonatology
Area of work

- Neonatology is a subspecialty of paediatrics that consists of the medical care of new-born infants, especially the ill or premature new-born infant
- It is a hospital-based specialty, and is usually practiced in neonatal intensive care units (NICUs)
- The principal patients of neonatologists are new-born infants who are ill or requiring special medical care due to prematurity, low birth weight, intrauterine growth retardation, congenital malformations (birth defects), sepsis and pulmonary hyperplasia or birth asphyxias

Scope

- Clinics, Hospitals, Universities and Private consultation

Nephrology
Area of work

- Nephrology is a specialty of medicine and paediatrics that concerns itself with the study of normal kidney function, kidney problems, the treatment of kidney problems, dialysis and kidney transplantation

- Systemic conditions that affect the kidneys (such as diabetes and autoimmune disease) and systemic problems that occur as a result of kidney problems (such as renal osteodystrophy and hypertension) are also studied in nephrology
- A physician who has undertaken additional training to become an expert in nephrology may call themselves a nephrologist or renal physician

Scope

- Clinics, Hospitals, Universities and Private consultation

Neurological Surgery
Area of work

- Prevention, diagnosis, evaluation, treatment, critical care and rehabilitation of disorders of the central, peripheral and autonomic nervous systems including their supporting structures and vascular supply
- Evaluation and treatment of pathological processes which modify function or activity of the nervous system
- Operative and non-operative management of pain
- Neurological surgery involves the surgical, non-surgical and stereotactic radio surgical treatment of adult and paediatric patients with disorders of the

  - o Nervous system
  - o Brain
  - o Meninges
  - o Skull
  - o Skull base
  - o Intracranial and extra cranial vasculature supplying the brain and spinal cord
  - o Pituitary gland
  - o Spinal cord
  - o Cranial, peripheral and spinal nerves throughout their distribution

Scope

- Clinics, Hospitals, Universities and Private consultation

Neurology
Area of work

- Diagnosis and treatment of all types of disease or impaired function of the brain, spinal cord, peripheral nerves, muscles and autonomic nervous system as well as the blood vessels that relate to these structures
- Neurologists can receive training in the following subspecialties:

  o Clinical neurophysiology, which involves specialization in the diagnosis and management of central, peripheral and autonomic nervous system disorders using a combination of clinical evaluation and electrophysiological testing such as electroencephalography (EEG), electromyography (EMG) and nerve conduction studies (NCS) among others

  o Hospice and palliative medicine, which involves preventing and relieving the suffering experienced by patients with life-limiting illness

  o Neurodevelopment disabilities, which involves diagnosing and managing chronic conditions that affect the developing and mature nervous system such as cerebral palsy, mental retardation, and chronic behavioural syndromes or neurologic conditions

  o Neuromuscular medicine, which involves diagnosing and managing disorders of nerves, muscle or neuromuscular junction

  o Pain medicine, which involves providing a high level of care, either as a primary physician or consultant, for patients experiencing problems with acute, chronic or cancer pain in hospital and ambulatory settings

  o Sleep medicine, which involves diagnosing and managing of clinical conditions that occur during sleep, disturb sleep or are affected by disturbances in the wake-sleep cycle

  o Vascular neurology, which involves evaluating, preventing, treating and recovering from vascular diseases of the nervous system

Scope

- Clinics, Hospitals, Universities and Private consultation

Nuclear Medicine
Area of work

- Use the tracer principle to evaluate molecular, metabolic, physiologic and pathologic conditions of the body for the purposes of diagnosis, therapy and research
- Nuclear medicine encompasses molecular imaging to detect the tracer signal to provide spatial and temporal information on the processes of interest to evaluate a wide variety of diseases
- The nuclear medicine physician often uses anatomic imaging combined with molecular imaging (e.g., PET/CT)
- The most common diagnostic applications of nuclear medicine include the early detection of coronary artery disease, cancer diagnosis and staging, and the evaluation of the effect of cancer treatment

Scope

- Clinics, Hospitals, Universities and Private consultation

Nursing
Area of work

- Giving the patients their medications on time, reporting to the doctors about health of the patient, taking care of stock in the hospital ward etc
- There are different types of nurses that include:
    - o Acute Care Nurse
    - o Ambulatory Care Nurse
    - o Community Health Nurse
    - o Critical Care Nurse
    - o Emergency Nurse
    - o Geriatrics Nurse
    - o Licensed Practical Nurse
    - o Maternity Nurse
    - o Nursing, Psychiatric and Home Health Aides
    - o Occupational Health Nurse
    - o Operating Room Nurse
    - o Paediatrics Nurse
    - o Psychiatry Nurse
    - o Registered/Certified Nurses and Nursing Assistants

Scope

- Clinics, Hospitals, Universities and Private consultation

Obstetrics and Gynaecology
Area of work

- An obstetrician/gynaecologist possesses special knowledge, skills and professional capability in the medical and surgical care of the female reproductive system and associated disorders
- Serves as a consultant to other physicians and as a primary physician for women
- Obstetrician/gynaecologists can receive training in the following subspecialties:
  - Critical care medicine, which involves diagnosing, treating, and supporting female patients with multiple organ dysfunctions
  - Gynaecologic oncology, which involves providing consultation and comprehensive management of patients with gynaecologic cancer
  - Hospice and palliative medicine, which involves preventing and relieving the suffering experienced by patients with life-limiting illnesses
  - Maternal and fetal medicine, which involves caring for, or providing consultation on, patients with complications of pregnancy
  - Reproductive endocrinology and infertility, which involves managing complex problems relating to reproductive endocrinology and infertility

Scope

- Clinics, Hospitals, Universities and Private consultation

Ophthalmology
Area of work

- Provide comprehensive eye and vision care for patients of all ages
- Diagnose, monitor and medically or surgically treat all ocular and visual disorders

- Provide consultative services for the diagnosis and management of ocular manifestation of systemic diseases such as diabetes, hypertension and infectious and non-infectious inflammation

Scope

- Clinics, Hospitals, Universities and Private consultation

Orthopaedic Surgery
Area of work

- Preservation, investigation and restoration of the form and function of the extremities, spine and associated structures by medical, surgical and physical means
- Involved with the care of patients whose musculoskeletal problems include congenital deformities, trauma, infections, tumours, metabolic disturbances of the musculoskeletal system, deformities, injuries
- Involved with the care of patients with degenerative diseases of the spine, hands, feet, knee, hip, shoulder, and elbow in children and adults
- Concerned with primary and secondary muscular problems and the effects of the central or peripheral nervous system lesions of the musculoskeletal system

Scope

- Clinics, Hospitals, Universities and Private consultation

Otolaryngology
Area of work

- An otolaryngologist is a head and neck surgeon who provides comprehensive medical and surgical care for patients with diseases and disorders that affect the ears, nose, throat, the respiratory and upper alimentary systems, and related structures of the head and neck
- Diagnose and provide medical and surgical therapy or prevention of diseases, allergies, neoplasms, deformities, disorders and injuries of the ears, nose, sinuses, throat, respiratory and upper alimentary systems, face, jaws and the other head and neck systems

- Otolaryngologists can receive training in the following subspecialties:

    o Neurotology, which involves treating diseases of the ear and temporal bone including disorders of hearing and balance
    o Paediatric otolaryngology, which involves diagnosing and treating children with diseases of the ear, nose and throat including disorders of voice, speech, language and hearing
    o Plastic surgery within the head and neck which involves plastic and reconstructive procedures within the head, face, neck and associated structures including cutaneous head and neck oncology and reconstruction, management of maxillofacial trauma, soft tissue repair and neural surgery
    o Sleep medicine, which involves diagnosing and managing clinical conditions that occur during sleep, disturb sleep or are affected by disturbances in the wake-sleep cycle

Scope

- Clinics, Hospitals, Universities and Private consultation

Pathology
Area of work

- This specialist uses information gathered from the microscopic examination of tissue specimens, cells, and body fluids, and from clinical laboratory tests on body fluids and secretions for the diagnosis, exclusion, and monitoring of disease
- Pathologists can receive training in the following subspecialties:

    o Blood banking/transfusion medicine
    o Chemical pathology
    o Cytopathology
    o Dermatopathology
    o Forensic pathology
    o Haematology
    o Medical microbiology
    o Molecular genetic pathology
    o Neuropathology
    o Paediatric pathology

Scope

- Clinics, Hospitals, Universities and Private consultation

Paediatrics
Area of work

- A paediatrician is concerned with the physical, emotional and social health of children from birth to young adulthood
- Care encompasses a broad spectrum of health services ranging from preventive health care to the diagnosis and treatment of acute and chronic diseases
- Deal with biological, social and environmental influences on the developing child and with the impact of disease and dysfunction on development
- Paediatricians can receive training in the following subspecialties:

  - o Adolescent medicine
  - o Developmental-behavioural paediatrics
  - o Hospice and palliative medicine
  - o Medical toxicology
  - o Neonatal-perinatal medicine
  - o Neurodevelopmental disabilities
  - o Paediatric cardiology
  - o Paediatric critical care medicine
  - o Paediatric emergency medicine
  - o Paediatric endocrinology
  - o Paediatric gastroenterology
  - o Paediatric haematology-oncology
  - o Paediatric infectious diseases
  - o Paediatric nephrology
  - o Paediatric pulmonology
  - o Paediatric rheumatology
  - o Paediatric sports medicine
  - o Paediatric transplant hepatology
  - o Sleep medicine

Scope

- Clinics, Hospitals, Universities and Private consultation

Physical Medicine and Rehabilitation
Area of work

- Evaluate, diagnose and treat patients with physical disabilities that may arise from conditions affecting the musculoskeletal system such as neck and back pain, sports injuries or other painful conditions
- A physician certified in physical medicine and rehabilitation is often called a physiatrist
- To achieve maximum restoration of physical, psychological, social and vocational function through comprehensive rehabilitation as well as effective pain management
- Physiatrists can receive training in the following subspecialties:

    o Hospice and palliative medicine, which involves preventing and relieving the suffering experienced by patients with life-limiting illnesses
    o Neuromuscular medicine, which requires specialized knowledge in the science, clinical evaluation and management of these disorders
    o Pain medicine, which involves providing a high level of care for patients experiencing problems with acute, chronic or cancer pain
    o Paediatric rehabilitation medicine, which involves preventing, diagnosing, treating and managing congenital and childhood-onset physical impairments
    o Spinal cord injury medicine, which addresses the prevention, diagnosis, treatment and management of traumatic spinal cord injury and non-traumatic causes of spinal cord dysfunction
    o Sports medicine, which entails continuous care related to the enhancement of health and fitness as well as the prevention of injury and illness

Scope

- Clinics, Hospitals, Universities and Private consultation

Plastic Surgery
Area of work

- Manages the repair, reconstruction or replacement of physical defects of form or function involving the skin, musculoskeletal system, head and facial structures, hands, extremities, breasts and trunk as well as cosmetic enhancement of these areas
- Uses cosmetic surgical principles to improve overall appearance and to optimize this outcome of reconstructive procedures
- Plastic surgeons can receive training in the following subspecialties:

    o Plastic surgery within the head and neck, which involves reconstructive treatment of disorders of the soft and hard tissues of the face and cranial areas
    o Surgery of the hand, which requires expertise in the investigation, preservation and restoration by medical, surgical and rehabilitative means, of all structures of the hand and wrist

Scope

- Clinics, Hospitals, Universities and Private consultation

Preventive Medicine
Area of work

- Focus on the health of individuals and defined populations to protect, promote and maintain health and well-being as well as to prevent disease, disability and premature death
- A preventive medicine physician may be a specialist in general preventive medicine, public health, occupational medicine or aerospace medicine
- Public health and general preventive medicine involves health promotion and disease prevention in communities and in defined populations
- Physicians in preventive medicine can receive training in the following subspecialty areas:

    o Medical toxicology, which involves evaluating and managing patients with accidental or purposeful poisoning through drugs or toxins o   Undersea and hyperbaric medicine, which involves the treatment of decompression illness and diving accident cases

Scope

- Clinics, Hospitals, Universities and Private consultation

Psychiatry
Area of work

- Prevention, diagnosis and treatment of mental, addictive and emotional disorders such as schizophrenia and other psychotic disorders, mood disorders, anxiety disorders, substance-related disorders, sexual and gender identity disorders and adjustment disorders
- Understand the biologic, psychological and social components of illness, and therefore uniquely treat the whole person
- A psychiatrist is qualified to order diagnostic laboratory tests and to prescribe medications, evaluate and treat psychological and interpersonal problems, and to intervene with families who are coping with stress, crises and other problems in living
- Psychiatrists can receive training in the following subspecialties:

    o   Addiction psychiatry
    o   Child and adolescent psychiatry
    o   Clinical neurophysiology
    o   Forensic psychiatry
    o   Geriatric psychiatry
    o   Hospice and palliative medicine
    o   Pain management
    o   Psychosomatic medicine
    o   Sleep medicine

Scope

- Clinics, Hospitals, Universities and Private consultation

Radiation Oncology
Area of work

- Therapeutic application of radiant energy and its modifiers as well as the study and management of disease, especially malignant tumours
- Radiation oncologists can receive training in the following subspecialty:

    o Hospice and palliative medicine, which involves preventing and relieving the suffering experienced by patients with life-limiting illnesses

Scope

- Clinics, Hospitals, Universities and Private consultation

Radiology
Area of work

- Utilize imaging methodologies to diagnose and manage patients and provide therapeutic options
- Utilize x-ray, ionizing radiation, radionuclides, ultrasound, electromagnetic radiation and image-guided intervention to diagnose and treat disease
- Physicians practicing in the field of radiology specialize in diagnostic radiology or radiation oncology
- Radiologists can receive training in the following subspecialties:

    o Neuroradiology
    o Nuclear radiology
    o Paediatric radiology
    o Vascular and interventional radiology

Scope

- Clinics, Hospitals, Universities and Private consultation

Rheumatology
Area of work

- Diagnosis and therapy of rheumatic diseases

- Deal mainly with clinical problems involving joints, soft tissues, autoimmune diseases, vasculitis and heritable connective tissue disorders
- Rheumatologists treat arthritis, autoimmune diseases, pain disorders affecting joints and osteoporosis
- There are more than 200 types of these diseases, including rheumatoid arthritis, osteoarthritis, gout, lupus, back pain, osteoporosis and tendinitis

Scope

Clinics, Hospitals, Universities and Private consultation

Therapy and rehabilitation
Area of work

- Help patients learn and develop skills related to daily living and self-care
- Work with patients and monitor their progress
- Most of these patients are children with a genetic disorder that needs therapy, people with disabilities or restriction of movement due to accidents or paralysis etc
- They work in hospitals, nursing homes, private clinics and as well as give home visits
- The therapy and rehabilitation careers list is as follows:

  o Occupational Therapist
  o Occupational Therapy Assistant
  o Physical Therapist
  o Physical Therapist Assistant
  o Physiotherapists
  o Psychotherapist
  o Therapeutic Recreation Specialist

Scope

Clinics, Hospitals, Universities and Private consultation

Thoracic Surgery/Cardiologist
Area of work

- Provides the operative, perioperative care and critical care of patients with acquired and congenital pathologic conditions within the chest, surgical repair of heart lesions as well as congenital and acquired conditions of the heart, including the pericardium, coronary arteries, valves and myocardium
- Includes pathologic conditions of the lung, oesophagus, and chest wall
- Includes abnormalities of the great vessels, tumours of the mediastinum
- Includes diseases of the diaphragm and pericardium
- Management of the airway and injuries of the chest are within the scope of the specialty
- Thoracic surgeons can receive training in the following subspecialty:

  o Congenital cardiac surgery, which involves operative treatment of structural abnormalities involving the heart and major blood vessels

Scope

Clinics, Hospitals, Universities and Private consultation

Urology
Area of work

- Manage congenital and acquired conditions of the genitourinary system and contiguous structures including the adrenal gland
- Skilled in medical and open surgical therapy of these conditions as well as endoscopic, percutaneous and other minimally invasive methods

Scope

Clinics, Hospitals, Universities and Private consultation

Veterinary physician
Area of work

- Treat disease, disorder and injury in non-human animals
- Involved in a general practice, treating animals of all types
- May be specialised in a specific group of animals such as companion animals, livestock, zoo animals or horses; or may specialise in a narrow medical discipline such as surgery, dermatology or internal medicine

Scope

Clinics, Hospitals, Universities and Private consultation

Vision Associated Professions
Area of work

- Help correct vision problems of patients and help them see well
- The vision associated professionals under this group are as follows:

  o Ophthalmologist
  o Ophthalmic Assistant/Technician/Technologist
  o Ophthalmic Dispensing Optician
  o Optometrist
  o Orientation and Mobility Specialist
  o Orthoptist
  o Teacher of the Visually Impaired
  o Vision Rehabilitation Therapist
  o Optician

Scope

Clinics, Hospitals, Universities and Private consultation

Other Science Careers

Science stream offers many other career options also to students not opting for engineering and medical careers. Some of the choices available are:

Bachelor degree in Architecture (B Arch)
Area of work

- Deal with planning, designing and construction of building and structures like houses, apartments, offices and industrial complexes, hospitals, hotels, airport terminals, stadiums, commercial complexes, schools etc
- Specializations in Architecture can be divided into industrial design, urban design, landscape architecture, town planning, environmental planning, building engineering and transport planning etc

Scope

- Construction related industries
- Architectural firms and companies
- Government agencies responsible for renovating and preserving ancient/historical structures
- House movers and planning bodies
- Structural consultants
- Hazard control and rehabilitation agencies

B. Sc. Agriculture
Area of work

- Production of food grains, vegetables and fruits and allied activities like dairying, poultry farming and horticulture
- Can opt for wide range of options in agricultural sectors including research, teaching, inspection and commercial activities of establishing farms, plantations, orchards and carrying on exports of produce from them

Scope

- Actuarial Analyst-Agriculture
- Sales Officer-Agriculture/Instrumentation
- Agriculture Portfolio Manager
- Program Manager-Agriculture
- Research/Fundamental Analyst (Agriculture commodities)
- Primary Production Managers (Expert Agriculture)
- Farming Consultant/Agronomist
- Associate Manager-Strategic Planning

- Agriculture Officer
- Manager-Manufacturing (Agricultural Tractors)
- Agricultural Lecturer
- Subject Matter Specialist-Agriculture
- Management Executive (Agriculture)
- Agriculture officer-Rural Housing Finance
- Sales Executive/Manager (Chemical, Agriculture, Pesticides)
- Sales Manager-Agricultural Products
- Marketing Executive-Agriculture
- Project Manager-Plantation Establishment

Bachelor degree in Science (B Sc)
Area of work

- A three year degree in which physics, chemistry and maths/ biology are taught
- After B.Sc., you can opt for Master of Science (M.Sc.)
- Science includes various subjects like Biotechnology, Biology, Botany, Microbiology, Chemistry, Physics, Mathematics, Zoology and Computer Science etc

Scope

- Agriculture Industry
- Aquariums
- Biotechnology Firms
- Chemical Industry
- Educational Institutes
- Environmental Management and Conservation
- Forensic Crime Research
- Food Institutes
- Forest Services
- Geological Survey Departments
- Health Care Providers
- Hospitals
- Industrial Laboratories
- Oil Industry
- Pharmaceuticals and Biotechnology Industry
- Research Firms
- Seed and Nursery Companies
- Space Research Institutes
- Testing Laboratories

- Wildlife and Fishery Departments
- Waste-water Plants

B Sc in Electronics and Communication
Area of work

- This course focuses on advanced experimental technical skills in electronics field
- After completion of this course, students are eligible to work as Electronic Service Engineer/Electronic hardware and Software Engineer/Maintenance Engineer etc

Scope

- Indian Telephone Industries
- Civil Aviation
- Development Centres in various States
- Defence
- NPL
- A.I.R
- Posts and Telegraph Department
- Railways
- Bharat Electronics Limited
- D.R.D.O
- Telecommunication
- Software Engineering/IT
- Power sector
- Hardware Manufacturing
- Home Appliance and VLSI design
- Television Industry
- Research & Development

B Sc in Statistics
Area of work

- Students with a degree in B.Sc. Statistics are eligible to apply for various jobs in Banking, IT, Quality control etc
- They can take up Actuarial Science as a specialization and join in various financial and share trading companies
- A student with Masters or Ph.D. in Statistics can apply for jobs such as a business analyst, statistics lecturer, professor etc

- They can also go for jobs like software engineer, investigative officer, statistics analyst, researcher etc

Scope

- Market Research Analyst-Good in Statistics
- Subject Matter Expert-Statistics
- Assistant Professor-Statistics
- Content Writer-Statistics
- Trainer-Statistics
- Analysis/Statistics Manager
- Online Statistics Tutor
- Consultant-Statistics
- Actuary Manager-M.Sc. Statistics
- Assistant Manager Human Resource
- Assistant Manager-Research and marketing
- Credit Risk Strategist
- The SSC also carries out a recruitment process as to appoint eligible candidates in to the Statistical Investigators post
- The Private sector also require qualified Statisticians in the Insurance, IT and software fields
- Some of the most renowned global Statistical Organizations are Euro-stat, IAOS, OECD, PARIS21 and UNESCO

B Sc in Animation
Area of work

- Advertising field—Product designer, Animator, Modeller, Compositor, Editor, Film-Story board artist, Character modeller, Character Animator, Texturing artist, Rigging artist, Compositor, Editor, VFX, Tilling animator, Camera Tracking, Wire removal artist. Gaming-character modeller, Character Animator, Texture artist, VFX, Programmer
- Educational Content Development-3D Software developer, animator (2D & 3D) for developing Rhymes CD, Encyclopaedia, Subject CD's, Simulators, Medical Animation

Scope

- 2D/3D Animator
- Graphic Designer
- 3D Modeller

- Web Designer
- Multimedia Programmer
- Compositor
- 2D/3D Designer
- Visualizer
- AV Editor
- Content Developer
- Technical Trainer
- Pre and Post-Production Executive

B Sc in Aviation
Area of work

- Work area range from airline and airport management to air transport consultancy, to roles with industry suppliers and manufacturers, or international logistics
- Example destinations include airport or airline network development, operational and emergency planning, airport planning, design and development, air traffic forecasting and strategy

Scope

- Tourism departments
- Airlines
- Travel companies
- Job opportunities in Domestic/International Airlines in India and Abroad

B.Sc. in Economics
Area of work

- Research Analyst (Macro-Economic)
- Analyst-Economics & Strategy
- Data Entry Operator-Economics
- Content Developer/Subject Matter Experts-Economics
- Subject Matter Expert-Accounts/Economics
- Economics Teacher
- Senior Technical Assistant (Economics)
- Manager-Health Economics Modelling
- Guest Teachers-Department of Economics

Scope

- Government and non-government organizations
- Organizations such as FICCI, Ascham, CII, and PHDCCI hire economics experts
- Indian Economic Services can be pursued to get placed at the highest echelons in Commission, Planning Board, Ministry of Economic Affairs, National Sample Survey and other departments that need specialists in economics

B Sc in Environment & Botany
Area of work

- Can attain knowledge about growth, structure, development, re-production and metabolism of various species of plants and different methods of solving environmental problems and conservation
- Can work as ecologists, environment consultants, conservationists, plant explorers, farming consultant, forester, taxonomist, nursery manager etc

Scope

- Agriculture Industry
- Distilleries
- Fertilizer Plants
- Food Processing Industries
- Forest and Environment Department
- Mines
- NGOs
- Pollution Control Boards
- Refineries
- Textile Mills
- Universities
- Urban Planning Commissions
- Waste Treatment Industries
- Water Resources Management Companies

B Sc in Forestry
Area of work

- Auditor—Forestry

- Assistant Manager—Forestry/Wildlife
- Nursery Manager
- Credit Manager—Retail Agri. Credit
- Farming Manager
- Teacher & Lecturer

Scope

- Government departments like department of forest and wildlife
- NGOs working in conservation and up-gradation of forests
- Research work in public sector research institutions like Indian Council of Forestry Research and Education (ICFRE), Institute of Social Forestry and Eco-rehabilitation and Wildlife Research Institutes
- Botanical and Zoological parts, Wildlife sanctuaries and National parks
- Universities
- Still photography, Film making and Wildlife journalism
- Television channels like Discovery and Natural Geographic
- Private consultancy in environmental impact assessment of large projects
- Organizations like World Wildlife Fund (WWF), Centre for Environment Education, Tata Energy Research Institute (TERI) and consultancy firms like Ernst and Young and KPMG

B Sc in Geology
Area of work

- Geology is the study of the earth, its processes, materials, history, structure and effects on organisms inhabited on earth.
- Includes geophysics, atmospheric science, oceanography, hydrogeology, palaeontology, crystallography, geo-statistics, etc
- Can work as

  o Executive Trainee-Geology
  o Manager-Geology
  o Geologists
  o Project Assistant/Project Fellow
  o Deputy Adviser (Minerals)
  o Technical Analyst
  o Assist. Soil Scientist
  o Manager-Marketing

o Head-Mine Planning
o Research Associate

Scope

- You can work with the Geological Survey of India, groundwater authorities, mining departments, mining companies, oil and exploration companies, pollution control boards and various research organisations

B Sc in Horticulture
Area of work

- Horticulture is related to cultivation of vegetables, fruits, flowers, crops, tuber crops and medicinal, aromatic and ornamental plants
- Can attain knowledge about crop production, plant propagation, plant breeding, and genetic engineering, preparation of soil and plant physiology and biochemistry
- Can work in various fields including floral design, garden centres, teaching, fruit and vegetable production, arboriculture, landscape construction etc

Scope

- Actuarial Analyst-Agriculture
- Sales Officer-Agriculture/Instrumentation
- Agriculture Portfolio Manager
- Program Manager-Agriculture
- Research/Fundamental Analyst (Agriculture commodities)
- Primary Production Managers (Expert Agriculture)
- Farming Consultant/Agronomist
- Associate Manager-Strategic Planning
- Agriculture Officer
- Manager-Manufacturing (Agricultural Tractors)
- Agricultural Lecturer
- Subject Matter Specialist-Agriculture
- Management Executive (Agriculture)
- Agriculture officer-Rural Housing Finance
- Sales Executive/Manager (Chemical, Agriculture, Pesticides)
- Sales Manager-Agricultural Products
- Marketing Executive-Agriculture
- Project Manager-Plantation Establishment

B Sc in Information Technology
Area of work

- Focused on subjects such as software, databases and networking
- Focus on the mathematical and theoretical foundations of computing rather than emphasizing specific technologies
- This degree is awarded for completing a program of study in the field of software development, software testing, software engineering, web design, databases, programming, and computer networking and computer system

Scope

- Network Designer
- Network Administrator
- Security Analyst
- Telecommunication Engineer
- Information Security Engineer
- Network Consultant
- Security Policy Maker (Network)
- Project Manager
- Client/Server Specialist
- Lead Programmer

B Sc in Physics
Area of work

- Can join BARC as a scientific assistance
- Can join defence services
- Can go for M.Sc., after that can join research centres or lectureship

Scope

- Lab Supervisor
- Researcher
- Technician
- Teacher
- Scientists
- Consulting Physicist
- Senior Physicist
- Statistician

- Accountant
- Technical Writer
- Loan Officer
- Treasury Management Specialist

B Sc in Psychology
Area of work

- Psychology is the study of the mind, occurring partly via the study of behaviour and mental functions
- B.Sc. (Psychology) degree course involves study of mind processes, motives, reactions, feelings, conflict resolution, crisis management, groupthink, motivation and nature of mind

Scope

- Counselling Psychology
- Educational Psychology
- Forensic/Criminal Psychology
- Health Psychology
- Occupational Psychology
- Sport and Exercise Psychology
- Further & Higher Education Psychology Teaching
- Case Management
- Career Counsellor
- Re-habitation Specialist
- Psychiatric Technician

B Sc in Wildlife
Area of work

- The course lays its strong foundation on preserving the natural reserves of wildlife and forests of a nation
- There are a numerous job profiles which eagerly wait for the candidates with a degree of B.Sc. in wildlife
- The individuals can be employed as foresters, entomologists or dendrologists and a lot more in this series
- They can also prefer the versatile fields of silviculture, as forest range officers or as zoo curators
- An individual can also become an ethologist with this degree
- The individuals can also go for job prospects in the education sector

Scope

- Agriculture Industry
- Distilleries
- Fertilizer Plants
- Food Processing Industries
- Forest and Environment Department
- Mines
- NGOs
- Pollution Control Boards
- Refineries
- Textile Mills
- Universities
- Urban Planning Commissions
- Waste Treatment Industries
- Water Resources Management Companies

B Sc in Yoga
Area of work

- Run their own Yoga Centres
- Introduce yoga in higher secondary schools

Scope

- Research Officer-Yoga & Naturopathy
- Yoga Aerobics Instructor
- Assistant Ayurvedic Doctor
- Clinical Psychologist
- YOGA Therapist
- Yoga Instructor
- Yoga Teacher
- Therapists & Naturopaths
- Trainer/Instructor-Health Club

B Sc in Zoology
Area of work

- Zoology is branch of science related to study of living and extinct animals and their interaction with environment
- Wildlife biology, wildlife management and wildlife rehabilitation are related to this science

- You can gain knowledge about structure of organisms, certain forms of animals, their body functions, structures, habits, evolution and characteristics
- You can be zoologist, taxonomists, ornithologists, ichthyologists, lecturer, curator or educator

Scope

- Botany/Zoology Faculty Member
- Clinical Business Associate
- Clinical Business Associate
- Area Sales Manager
- Online Tutoring
- Research Associate
- Nutrition Specialist
- Medical Representative

B Sc in Computer Science
Area of work

- Specially designed for students looking for a career in computers
- The course covers all aspects of computers right from the basic fundamentals of computers to database systems & advanced courses like C++, Java etc
- Students can pursue further studies in M.Sc. or MCA or MCM and follow it up through research or take up Jobs as trainee programmers within the IT Industry

Scope

- Computers and Related Electronic Equipment Manufacturers
- Desktop Publishing
- Software Development Companies
- Banks
- Consultancies
- Financial Institutions
- Insurance Providers
- Schools and Colleges
- Government Agencies

B Sc in Archaeology
Area of work

- Archaeology is study of past human society and behaviour through excavation and analysis of fossils, building ruins, food grains, texts etc
- Under this course you can learn about museology, epigraphy, numismatics, archives and study of coins, fossils, inscriptions, manuscripts etc
- There are numerous career options both in India and abroad
- You can work as Archaeologists, Heritage Conservators, Numismatists, Archivists, Epigraphists, curators or lecturer

Scope

- Anthropological Survey of India
- Art Galleries
- Commission for Scheduled Castes
- Commission for Schedule Tribes
- Criminal Investigation Departments
- Documentary Film Companies
- Historical Societies
- Human Resource Departments of Corporate Houses and Industries
- Insurance Companies
- Libraries
- Minority Commission
- Museums
- Non-Governmental Organizations (NGOs)
- Other Backward Classes Commission
- Planning Commission
- United Nations Educational, Scientific and Cultural Organization (UNESCO)
- United Nations International Children's Emergency Fund (UNICEF)
- World Health Organization (WHO)

Bachelor in Computer Applications (BCA)
Area of work

- Bachelor of Computers Application (BCA) followed by a Master in Business Administration (MBA) or Master in Computer

Application (MCA) is one of the favoured paths for those seeking a career in the field of Information Technology (IT)

- IT has become an integral department in almost all corporate offices and this makes having an MBA/MCA a viable choice
- Not only in India, there is a huge demand for IT professionals throughout the world too
- Have various career options available like:

  o Book Keepers
  o Budget Analysts
  o Finance Managers
  o Teacher & lecturer
  o Marketing Managers
  o Business Consultants
  o Actuaries
  o Chief Information Officer
  o Computer Programmers
  o Computer Training
  o Computer Systems Analysts
  o Computer Scientists
  o Computer Support Service Specialist
  o Computer Presentation Specialist
  o Commercial and Industrial Designers
  o Database Administrators
  o Independent Consultants
  o Information Systems Manager
  o Project Manager
  o Systems Administrators
  o Software Developers
  o Software Publishers

Scope

- Multi-national companies
- Banks and other financial institutions
- Colleges and Universities
- Private and government organizations

Bachelor in hotel management (BHM)
Area of work

- It is a degree in Hotel Management and Catering Technology which is an undergraduate course for those who want to be in the glamorous service industry and like interacting with people
- Have various career options available like:

    o Hospitality Executive
    o Catering Officers
    o Catering Supervisors & Assistants
    o Hotel Management & Food Craft Institutes
    o Cabin Crew & Hostess & Host
    o Marketing & Sales Executives in
    o Manager and Director
    o Head & Manager
    o Marketing Manager

Scope

- Hotels and Restaurants
- Colleges and Universities
- Private and Government Institutions

B Sc in Genetics
Area of work

- Disease Control
- Hormone and Protein Synthesis
- Animal Research
- Medical Investigations of Gene Structure

Scope

- Animal Breeding Industry
- Animal Science
- Beauty Care
- Brewing
- Educational Institutions
- Food Processing Industry
- Genetic Testing
- Health Care

- Hormone and Protein Synthesis
- Horticulture
- Research and Development Institutes
- Agricultural Firms
- Biotechnology Industries
- Consultancies
- DNA Forensics Department
- Gene Therapy
- Hospitals
- Military
- Pharmaceutical Industry and Suppliers
- Universities

B Sc in Geography
Area of work

- After completing BSc in Geography there are many options for you
    - Post-graduation (MSc in Geography)
    - MBA
    - Geographic Information system
    - Join defence services
    - Become a teacher

- Career options available in this field are:
    - Urban Planner or Community Development
    - Cartographer
    - GIS Specialist
    - Climatologist
    - Environmental Management
    - Writer or Researcher
    - Demographer
    - National Park Service Ranger
    - Geo Analyst Trainee
    - Geography Teacher

Scope

- Private and government organizations
- Government jobs
- Colleges and universities

Merchant Navy
Area of work

- Merchant Navy refers to the merchant (commercial) fleet or ships of a country that transport cargo & passengers
- This fleet usually consists of passenger vessels, cargo liners, tankers, refrigerator ships etc
- It's a glamorous career option as it offers a heady mix of excellent pay, steady growth & constant travelling to exotic locales
- One should not confuse merchant navy with Indian navy

Scope

- Shipping companies is Govt and private sector

Arts Stream

Arts stream is generally preferred by students who want to make their career in politics, civil services and other services related to social work, public administration etc. But there are lots of other career options also available for students in this stream. Some of the choices available for students are:

Bachelor of Arts (General)
Area of work

- There are a wide range of opportunities for the students opting for this course
- Some of the fields to choose from are journalism, advertising, management, marketing, administration, politics, public services, teaching, psychology etc.

Scope

- Advertisement Industry
- Broadcasting Companies
- Business Process Outsourcing Units
- Civil Services
- Community Service
- Film Editing and Direction
- Graphics and Printing Industry
- International Relations
- Journalism and Mass Communication

- Law
- Library and Information Science
- Professional Writing
- Public Administration
- Public Planning
- Religious Studies
- Social Work

Bachelor of Arts (Advertising and Brand Management)
Area of work

- Advertising sale along with brand management and promotion
- Covers a deep analysis of the several planning campaign
- Practicing of strategies involving even management and sales promotion
- Various career options available under this field are:
    - Manager-Advertising and Brand
    - Assistant Brand Manager
    - Account Executive-Online Brand Management
    - Marketing Executive/Brand Management
    - Branding Manager-Marketing
    - Manager-Brand Marketing
    - Advertising Intern/Trainee
    - Business Development Executive
    - Sales Executive-Advertising
    - Client Servicing/Key Account Manager

Scope

- Advertisement Industry
- Marketing Companies
- Private and Government institutions
- Multi-national companies
- Banks and other financial institutions

Bachelor of Arts (Agro Services)
Area of work

- Usage and knowledge about agricultural equipment including balers, tractors, combine harvesters, windrowers and several short lines and equipment to service specialty or regional agricultural markets

- Various careers available under this field are:

  o Agriculture Commodity Analyst (technical)
  o Associate Tech. Leader-Agriculture/Tractor Industry
  o Regional Sales Manager
  o Program Manager-Agriculture
  o Recruitment Service Manager
  o Agronomist-Rice
  o Agriculture Portfolio Manager
  o Market Service Manager-Agriculture
  o Assistant Manager-Corporate Lease & Loans
  o Jr. Manager-Seed Production
  o Manager-Sales Planning-Branding

Scope

- Agriculture Firms
- Fertilizer Firms
- Agro based Industry
- Government Jobs
- Private and Govt companies
- Colleges and Universities

Bachelor of Arts (Ancient History)
Area of work

- Ancient history is the study of the written past from the beginning of recorded human history to the middle ages and the span of recorded history is roughly 5,000 years
- Various careers available under this field are:

  o History Teacher
  o Consultant-Curriculum Design (History)
  o Data History Analyst
  o Assistant Professor-History
  o Subject Matter Expert-History
  o Junior Research Fellows

Scope

- History Teacher
- Consultant-Curriculum Design (History)
- Data History Analyst

- Assistant Professor-History
- Subject Matter Expert-History
- Junior Research Fellows

Bachelor of Arts (Anthropology)
Area of work

- Study of the evolution of man and also the socio-cultural development of humans
- Covers the study of several branches of anthropology (Socio-cultural, Biological-Physical, Applied, Linguistic and Archaeological) that deals with various aspects of human developments

Scope

- Anthropological Survey of India
- Art Galleries
- Commission for Scheduled Castes
- Commission for Schedule Tribes
- Conservation Organizations
- Documentary Film Companies
- Human Resource Departments of Corporate Houses and Industries
- Minority Commission
- Non-Governmental Organizations (NGOs)
- Other Backward Classes Commission World Health Organization (WHO)
- B.A. Anthropology Job Types
- Archaeologists
- Archivists
- Culture Resource Managers
- Curators
- Linguists
- Research Scholar
- Social Workers in Media Houses
- Tour Guides
- Urban Planners

Bachelor of Arts (Arabic)
Area of work

- Covers the areas regarding Arabic literature: society, poetry, prose, drama, novels, grammar etc

Scope

- Arabic Translator
- Data Entry Clerk (Arabic)
- Arabic Translation (English to Arabic)
- Arabic Teacher
- Customer Care Job-Arabic Speaking
- Arabic Speaking-Call Centre
- Tutor for Arabic/Persian language
- Content Analyst/Language Specialist
- Language Analysts

Bachelor of Arts (Bengali)
Area of work

- Provides comprehensive knowledge about the Bangla language and its literature
- Covers studies of the Bengali literature, grammar and poetry

Scope

- Translator
- Junior Parliamentary Reporter
- Content Writer
- Faculty Teacher
- Trainer
- Data Entry Operator
- Call Centre Executive
- Tutor

Bachelor of Arts (Cinematography)
Area of work

- Explore the artistic creation of the moving image
- Explore the craft and technology of cinematography and videography to increase consistency and predictability and to enhance experimentation in the creation of the moving image
- Prepares individuals to communicate dramatic information, ideas, moods and feelings through the making and producing of films and videos

Scope

- Producers
- Directors
- Film editors
- Camera operators
- Lighting specialists

Bachelor of Arts (Communicative English)
Area of work

- Communicative English refers to that English which helps us to communicate effectively with people using language functions
- Proficiency in English is accepted to be an essential requirement for communication at national as well as international levels

Scope

- Trainer-Communicative English
- English Language Specialist
- English Trainer
- Assistant Professor-Language, Literature & Culture Studies
- Teacher & lecturer

Bachelor of Arts (Computer Science)
Area of work

- Focuses on mathematical and theoretical foundations of computing, rather than teaching specific technologies
- This degree is given for completing a program of study in the field of software development, software testing, software engineering, computer networking, web design, databases and programming
- The computer science or computing science is the same comprising the study of the theoretical foundations of information and computation and of practical techniques for their implementation and application in computer systems

Scope

- Lecturer-Computer Science
- Assistant Professor-Computer Science

- Teacher-Computer Science
- Back Office Executive-Computer Science
- Vocational Instructor-Computer Science
- Computer Operator
- Computer Programmer Operator
- Data Entry Operator
- Technical Assistant-Computer
- Computer Lab Assistance

Bachelor of Arts (Defence & Strategic Studies)
Area of work

- Covers the study of Geopolitics and Military Geography, Science and Technology, Economics of Defence, Conflict Management and Conflict Resolution, International law, International Relations, Science and Technology, Area Studies, Nuclear policies etc

Scope

- Embedded Systems Architect-Defence Practice
- Hardware and Systems Professional (Avionics/Defence)
- Delivery Head-Defence
- Sales Manager-Defence Industry
- Quality Inspector-Leading Defence/Aerospace Client
- Manager Project Civil-Defence/Enviro Business
- Regional Service Mgr.-Defence Vehicles
- Associate Partner-Defence Channel
- Sales/BD-Government-Police/Paramilitary/Defence
- Personal Security Officer (Ex-Defence)
- Account Manager-Army/Navy/Defence

Bachelor of Arts (Drawing and Painting)
Area of work

- Part of painting and drawing is the addition of texture, whether the piece is realistic or abstract. There are various kinds of textures in art and design. Actual or real textures are those that can be touched such as the smooth surface of a metal sculpture or the spiky surface of a cactus

Scope

- Drawing Teacher
- Draughtsman-Drawing
- Manager-Design/Drawing
- Painting Inspector
- Graphic Designer
- Spray Painter Technician
- Team Manager-Paint shop
- Decorative Painter

Bachelor of Arts (Economics)
Area of work

- Economics is the social science that analyses the production, distribution, and consumption of goods and services. The curriculum comprising the areas such as definition, nature, scope, concepts, utility, production, market, monopoly and other minor or major aspects of Economics

Scope

- Agricultural Companies
- Economic Research Institutions
- Analysis/Forecasting Firms
- Stock Exchanges
- Financial Information Firms
- Banks/Credit Unions/Caisse Populaires
- International Trade Companies
- Manufacturing Firms
- Statistical Research Firms
- Economist
- Economic Researcher
- Sales Analyst
- Investment Analyst
- Investment Administrator
- Financial Service Manager
- Securities Analyst Trainee
- Fixed Income Portfolio Manager
- Customer Profit Analyst

Bachelor of Arts (Education)
Area of work

- Education is the means through which the aims and habits of a group of people lives on from one generation to the next. It can be pursued either as a Regular Course or as a Distance Education Course, the duration being the same, unless mentioned by the institute

Scope

- Coaching Centres
- Education Consultancies
- Education Department
- Home Tuitions
- Museums
- Private Tuitions
- Publishing House
- Research and Development Agencies
- Schools
- Physical Education Teacher
- Associate Professor-Special Education
- Divisional Education Consultant
- Assistant Professor-Physical Education
- Overseas Education Consultant
- Education Coordinator
- Content Writer Education

Bachelor of Arts (English Literature)
Area of work

- English Literature course covers the study of English Literature and writings from the middle Ages to the 20th century. The degree course covers lessons on almost all the best-known and best loved writers such as Chaucer, Shakespeare, Swift, Milton, Jane Austen, Dickens and the list is countless

Scope

- Broadcasting
- Business Process Outsourcing Units
- Business Organizations
- Civil Services

- Communication Management
- Film and Video Production
- Film Editing and Direction
- Graphics and Printing Industry
- Local and International Call Centres
- Media & Entertainment Industry
- Theatre
- Teacher & lecturer
- Translator
- Copy Editor-English Literature
- Subject Matter Expert English Literature
- English Content Writer
- English Language Trainer
- Spoken English Trainer

Bachelor of Arts (Fine Arts)
Area of work

- Fine art or fine arts comprise art forms developed mainly for aesthetics or concept rather than practical application. This Fine Arts course enables students to learn the whole concept of pipelining of production in 2D and 3D animation with the incorporation of in-depth traditional concepts of drawing and painting

Scope

- Assistant Lecturer-Fine Arts
- Academic Research Editor-Arts and Humanities
- Graphic Designer
- Art Teacher
- Flash Animators
- Retail Sales Executive-Fine Arts
- Faculty/Lecturer-Graphics Designing
- Art Liaison Official

Bachelor of Arts (Geography)
Area of work

- Geography is the science which deals with the study of the Earth and its lands, features, inhabitants, and phenomena. However, modern geography is an all-encompassing discipline that foremost seeks to understand the Earth and all of its human and natural complexities not only where object are but how they have changed and come to be

Scope

- Content Developer-Geography
- MAP Consultant
- Unit Sales Manager-Geographical Structure
- Accountant Assistant at Geo-Chem. Laboratories
- Geography Teacher
- Subject Matter Expert-Geography
- Tech. Labs Researcher
- Advance Course in Geography

Bachelor of Arts (German)
Area of work

- It concerns with the field of arts and covers the areas regarding German literature: society, poetry, prose, drama, novels, grammar etc

Scope

- German Instructor
- Bilingual (German/English or Italian/English) Panel
- Language Specialist
- German Associate Producer
- Social Science Researcher
- On-line Teacher German
- Sr. Consultant
- Project Manager/Bilingual German Speaking
- Technical Account Manager
- Foreign Language Trainer
- Translator for MNCs and Government Organizations
- Diplomatic Service Professional
- Tourism Industry (Tour Guide)
- Freelance Writer, Translator, Interpreter

Bachelor of Arts (Hindi)
Area of work

- Hindi is a language made up of mostly Sanskrit language along with Urdu, etc. Hindi is the official language of India

Scope

- Consultant-Hindi Proof reading
- Teacher & Home Teacher
- Customer Service Associate
- Sales Coordinator-with Hindi
- Interpreter-from one language to other
- Content Writer-Editor (Hindi)
- Hindi Translator
- Part Time Trainer-Hindi
- Assistant Professor-Hindi Journalism
- Hindi Officer
- Data Entry Operator
- Tele-caller-Hindi

Bachelor of Arts (Home Science)
Area of work

- Home Science covers the study of nutrition, health and growth measures including the science that deals with the surroundings and environment. The degree course mainly comprise of the study of the major topics of Home Science like Food Science, Fundamentals of Resource Management, Foundations of Human Development, Introduction to Fabric and Apparel Science, Foundations of Food and Nutrition, etc

Scope

- Apparel Merchandising
- Cafeterias
- Commercial Restaurants
- Community Development Programs
- Consultancy and Counselling Centres
- Dress-Making
- Extension Education
- Fashion Designing
- Fashion Journalism
- Food Industry
- Food Preservation
- Hospitals
- Hotels
- Manufacturing Industries

- Sales Promotion of Food Items
- Specialized Cooking
- Textile Businesses
- Tourist Resorts
- Assistant Dress Designer
- Assistant Fashion Designer
- Baby Care Taker
- Child Care Giver
- Cook/Chef
- Demonstrator
- Food Analyst
- Food Scientist
- Health Care Worker
- Hospital Attendant
- Housekeeper
- Nanny
- Nutrition Expert
- Pantry In-charge
- Research Assistant

Bachelor of Arts (Mathematics)
Area of work

- Mathematics is the study of quantity, structure, space, and change
- Mathematicians seek out patterns and formulate new conjectures
- Mathematicians resolve the truth or falsity of conjectures by mathematical proofs, which are arguments sufficient to convince other mathematicians of their validity

Scope

- Treasury Management Specialist
- Technical Writer
- Researcher
- Loan Officer
- Economist
- Demographer
- Computer Programmer
- Aerodynamics Specialist
- Accountant
- Insurance Manager

Bachelor of Arts (Music)
Area of work

- Music comprises a combination of vocal music, instrumental music and various dance forms. The degree course involves the study of music theory, music interpretation, history of music, composing, voice instruction, etc

Scope

- Advertising Specialist
- Art Director
- Artist & Repertoire (A&R) Person
- Band Leader
- Composer/Arranger
- Concert Promoter
- Conductor
- Copy Writer
- Copyright Specialist
- Disc Jockey
- Film Music Director/Editor
- Manager
- Music Attorney
- Music Critic
- Music Publisher
- Music Software Programmer
- Music Teacher
- Musician
- Orchestra Librarian
- Producer
- Publicist
- Public Relations Specialist
- Publications Specialist
- Recording Technician
- Singer/Performer
- Studio Musician
- Technical Writer
- Tour Manager Writer/Music Journalist
- Advertising Agencies
- Booking and Talent Agencies
- Colleges and Universities
- Department of Cultural Affairs

- Department of Education
- Elementary and Secondary Schools
- Entertainment Companies
- Law Firms
- Magazines
- Media Firms
- Music and Film Studios
- Music and Video Stores
- Music Companies
- Music Industry Associations
- National Archives
- Newspapers
- Offices of International Education
- Orchestras and Bands
- Performing Arts Centres
- Production Companies
- Publishing Firms
- Public Relations Firms
- Travel and Tourism Departments

Bachelor of Arts (Philosophy)
Area of work

- It is the study of general and fundamental problems, such as those connected with existence, knowledge, values, reason, mind, and language

Scope

- Teaching
- Creative writing
- Editing and Publishing
- Mediation
- Public relations and journalism
- Philosophical Counselling/Philosophical Practice
- Teacher & Lecturer
- Novelist, Non-fiction Writer, or Poet
- Jobs of Communication Skills
- Mediators (as in divorce cases, or to settle disputes between unions and corporations)
- Public Relation Journalist
- Counsellor and Therapist

Bachelor of Arts (Political Science)
Area of work

- Political science is a social science concerned with the study of the state, government and politics; it deals extensively with the theory and practice of politics, and the analysis of political systems and political behaviour

Scope

- Public Relations Departments
- Colleges and Universities
- Consulting Firms
- Intelligence Wings
- Law Firms
- Public Policy Organisations
- Politics
- Diplomacy
- TV Channels
- Indian Civil Services
- Campaign Organiser
- Teacher & Professor
- Career Counsellor
- Corporate Public Affairs Advisor
- Advocate
- Budget Analyst
- Legislative Analyst
- Research Analyst
- Political Commentator
- IAS, IPS & PCS officers

Bachelor of Arts (Psychology)
Area of work

- Psychology is the scientific study of the mental and behavioural functions of humans and animals. Subjects usually studied under this degree are General Psychology, Statistics, Physiological Psychology, Social Psychology, Research Methods & Psychology Testing, Abnormal Psychology, development Psychology, Organizational Psychology, Child and Adolescent Psychology, Industrial Psychology etc

Scope

- Private industry
- Universities
- Schools & colleges
- Clinics
- Hospitals
- Government agencies
- Health centres, as assistant in administrative department and rehabilitation sector
- Counselling
- Social Work
- Human Resource Development
- Public Relations
- Academics and Research
- Advertising
- Market Research
- Personnel Training
- Civil Services

Bachelor of Arts (Sanskrit)

Area of work

- Sanskrit is a historical Indo-Aryan language and the primary liturgical language of Hinduism, Jainism and Buddhism. B.A. Honours in Sanskrit is chiefly about Sanskrit language and its literature

Scope

- Media
- Research
- Sales
- Education
- Business
- Tourism
- Law and Legal Jobs (translating work)
- Media and TV Jobs Writing and Publishing Jobs
- Reporter, Cameraman, Correspondent
- Data Observer & Collector
- Salesman, Customer Dealer, Purchaser
- Teacher, Trainer & Writer

- Sales Executive, Manager & Operator
- Guide & Translator
- Translator in Courts
- Operator or Orator in Sanskrit News Channels
- Poet, Novelist & Story Writer

Bachelor of Arts (Sociology)
Area of work

- Sociology is the study of society. It is a social science, a term with which it is sometimes synonymous, which uses various methods of empirical investigation and critical analysis to develop and refine a body of knowledge about human social activity

Scope

- Education Sector
- Corporations
- Criminal Justice Field
- Human Services
- Journalism
- Labour Unions
- Newspapers
- Prisons
- Radio Stations
- Trade Associations
- Research Organizations
- Teacher, Home Tutor & Lecturer
- Market Survey Researcher
- Criminal Justice Jobs-Corrections Officer, Juvenile
- Detention Officers, Court Officers
- Community Service Worker
- Journalist
- Labour Leader & Mediator
- Editorial Assistant
- Human Services Assistant
- Staff Reporter
- Training Advisor
- Census workers & Research Assistant

Bachelor of Arts (Public Administration)
Area of work

- The course comprises the study of various theories of Administration, Public Organisations, Public Services and the Constitutional framework. More clearly the B.A. (Public Administration) degree course teaches and trains the students in democratic values such as equality, justice, security and order

Scope

- Administrative Officer
- Consultant
- Corporate Manager
- Management Analyst
- Teacher
- Customs Inspector
- Labour Management Relations Specialist
- Personnel Management Specialist
- Social Worker
- Bureaucracy
- Economic Development
- Education
- Indian Civil Services
- Fire and Emergency Services
- Land Revenue Systems
- Corporate Management
- Municipal Bodies
- Panchayati Raj
- Police Department
- Public Works
- Secretariat
- Tribal Administration

Bachelor of Arts (Statistics)
Area of work

- Statistics includes study of the science of collection, organization, analysis, interpretation and presentation of numerical as well as categorical data. The B.A. (Statistics) degree course mainly covers the study of some of its specialized fields such as Actuarial Science, Applied Information Economics, Biostatistics, Business Statistics,

Data Analysis, Demography, Econometrics, Energy Statistics, Engineering Statistics, Psychological Statistics, Social Statistics, etc

Scope

- Assistant Professors
- Biometrician
- Biostatistician
- Data Analysts
- Data Interpreters
- Econometrician
- Enumerators
- Lecturers
- Research Analyst
- Research Scholars
- Statisticians
- Agricultural Research
- Banks
- Businesses
- Commerce
- Consulting Firms
- Data Survey Agencies
- Demographic Studies
- Economics
- Education
- Finance
- Indian Civil Services
- Indian Economic Services
- Indian Statistical Services
- Insurance
- Statistical and Economic Bureaus
- Statistical Research
- National Council of Applied Economic Research (NCAER)
- The Planning Commission

B.A. Travel and Tourism Management
Area of work

- Tourism Management is the study and analysis of the trends in the tourism industry. This course prepares the students with the skills, knowledge, and leadership qualities required to succeed as professionals in the tourism industry

121

Scope

- Airlines
- Travel agencies
- Tour operating companies
- Resorts
- Shipping companies
- Hotels
- State Tourism department
- Tour operators
- National and Regional Tourism Development Agencies
- Tourism marketing
- Tour guiding
- The airline industry
- Major tourist attractions
- Events management
- Research and business development

B.P.Ed.—Bachelor of Physical Education

Area of work

- It is an Undergraduate Academic Course dealing with the development and care for the human body. Physical Education Course is largely suited for sports persons or those who have a passion for sports and related activities. Non-sports person need to be energetic, enthusiastic and physically fit

Scope

- Sports and Business Marketing
- Sports Journalism
- Fitness Centre
- Sports Equipment Industries
- Colleges
- Private Schools
- Hotel Industries
- Sports Team
- Trainer/Instructor/Coach
- Sports Journalist
- Sports Goods Manufacture Marketing Executive
- Commentator
- Physical Education Instructors

- Umpire/Referee
- Professional Players
- Sport and Leisure Club Managers
- Administrative and Sports Duties
- Sports Photojournalists

Bachelor of Library and Information Science
Area of work

- It is an undergraduate Library Science course. Library and Information Science is associated with schools of library and information science
- Library science is a social science incorporating the humanities, law and applied science and studying topics related to libraries; the collection organization and the political economy of information

Scope

- Library Information Officer
- Officer (Library)
- Library Information Assistant
- Librarian/Assistant Librarian/Library Assistant
- Junior Library Attendant
- Assistant Technical Manager/Library Assistant/Technician
- Library Trainee
- Project Assistant
- Professional Assistant
- Storage Specialist
- Project Trainee

BA/LLB
Area of work

- Lawyers operate as advocates and advisors/solicitors. Advocates basically fight in court for rights of their client or they defend them against various cases.

Scope

- Banks
- Business houses

- Consultancies
- Educational institutes
- Judiciary
- News channels
- Newspapers
- Private practice
- Revenue department
- Sales tax and excise department
- State police department

Mass Communication/Journalism
Area of work

- Mass communication relate to the fields like public relations, communication, advertisement and journalism
- Mass Communication and journalism involves dissemination of information through reporting, writing, editing, broadcasting or cable casting news items though the print (magazines & newspapers) or electronic (television & web) media

Scope

- Advertising Agencies
- Books and Novels
- Broadcasting Corporations
- Central Information Service
- Circulation and Public Relations
- Journals
- Legal Affairs Department
- News Agencies
- Photography Companies
- Press Information Bureau
- Radio Telecasting Companies
- TV Channels
- AIR-All India Radio
- Newspapers
- Periodicals and Magazines
- Websites

Commerce Stream

Commerce stream is known for banking, finance, entrepreneurship, business administration and management careers. Students choosing this stream generally opt for careers related to business and banking. There are lots of opportunities available in this stream also and are described here.

Aviation and Hospitality Management
Area of work

- Work in the field of aviation, travel & hospitality
- There are lots of domestic as well as foreign career choices available in Aviation industry. Some of them are:

    o Air Traffic Controller
    o Airline Manager
    o Maintenance Manager
    o Safety Inspector
    o Passenger services Management
    o Fuel Management
    o Training Instructor
    o Base Manager
    o Cabin Crew
    o Commercial Pilot
    o Quality Control Manager
    o Cargo Officers

- Hospitality sector also offers lots of career choices as:

    o Kitchen Management
    o Housekeeping Management
    o Hotel Management

Scope

- College/Universities
- Professional development centres
- Tourism Board
- Airline Companies—domestic and foreign
- Hotel/Hospitals and other institutions
- Tourism Development Corporations and Resorts
- Fast Food chains

B. Com. (Honours in Finance)
Area of work

- The field of finance includes the study of financial markets, financial instruments, corporate finance, personal finance, banks & banking, financial regulation, international finance and related topics.
- Various positions offered to B.Com. Finance graduates are:

  o Accounts Assistant
  o Business Analyst
  o Equity Research Analyst
  o Corporate Analyst
  o Investments Analyst
  o Market Analyst
  o Marketing Manager
  o Securities Analyst
  o Senior Accountant
  o Operations Manager
  o Financial Analyst
  o Assistant Manager-Finance Accounting and Logistics
  o Associate-Finance/Accounting

Scope

- Colleges/Universities/Institutions
- Job in multi-national companies
- Jobs in investment companies, banks, financial institutions, stock trading, market research

B.Com. Business Economics
Area of work

- Business economics is a course in applied economics that also includes the training in essential skills in marketing and communication.
- Some of the job types for graduates with this course are as listed below:

  o Manager-Medical Economics
  o Economics Business Analyst
  o Business Analyst Deployment Economics
  o Teacher and Tutor

    o   Business Finance-Business Economics Associate
    o   Economics Business Manager
    o   Analyst-Business Planning & Finance
    o   Sr. Analyst-Business Analytics
    o   Marketing, Sales, Business Development Executives
    o   Business Manager-Analytics
    o   Business Analyst

Scope

- Insurance Sector
- Consultancies
- Banks
- Stock market
- Finance Companies
- Corporate Sector

B.B.A. (Bachelor in business administration)
Area of work

- Bachelor of Business Administration (BBA) is a bachelor's degree in business administration. Some of the similar courses are Bachelor in Management Studies (BMS), Bachelor of Business Management (BBM) & Bachelor of Business Studies (BBS). BBA is like an introductory course to MBA and is the under-graduate programme to take up if you are planning to pursue an MBA.

Scope

- Banks
- Insurance Industry
- Charity Associations
- Business Schools
- Savings and Loan Associations
- Credit Unions
- Mortgage Companies
- Finance Companies
- Consultancies
- Shopping Malls
- Management Consulting Firms
- Government Agencies
- Almost in all Large and Small Companies

B.B.A. Accounting & Finance
Area of work

- It is an undergraduate Commerce course. Account and Finance course is the study in accounting, financial planning, economics and other similar areas of operation in any organization or business
- Some of the job types are:
  - o Accounts & Finance Consultant
  - o Accounts Assistant with a Chartered Accountant
  - o Accounts Executive
  - o Accounts Officer
  - o Assistant Controller
  - o Business Analyst
  - o Equity Research Analyst
  - o Finance Executive
  - o Finance Officer
  - o Internal Auditor
  - o Personal Financial Adviser
  - o Research Analyst
  - o Tax Assistant
  - o Treasurer

Scope

- Banks
- Insurance Industry
- Charity Associations
- Business Schools
- Savings and Loan Associations
- Credit Unions
- Mortgage Companies
- Finance Companies
- Consultancies
- Shopping Malls

B.B.A. Banking
Area of work

- Includes the study of business management and related fields.

- Professional degree where theoretical concepts like management information systems, fundamentals of Human Resource Management (HRM), Financial Law and the fundamentals of marketing are taught.
- Some of the job types are:

    o Administrative Officer (AO)
    o Agent and Broker
    o Asset Manager
    o Assistant Administrative Officer (AAO)
    o Assistant Controller
    o Credit and Risk Manager
    o Customer Service Representative
    o Development Officer
    o Internal Auditor
    o Insurance Manager
    o Investment Analyst
    o Investment Banker
    o Loan Counsellor
    o Loss Control Specialist
    o Loan Officer
    o Marketing and Sales Executive
    o Marketing Manager
    o Personal Financial Advisor
    o Recovery Agent
    o Sales Representative
    o Sales Manager and Officer
    o Stock Analyst
    o Treasurer

Scope

- Public Sector Departments
- Educational Institutions
- Industrial Houses
- Banks
- Commercial Banks
- Investment Banking Houses
- Insurance Firms
- Accounting Firms
- Management Consulting Firms
- Government Agencies

- Large and Small Corporations

B.B.A. Banking & Finance
Area of work

- Banking and Finance is the course of study of concepts used in the banking and finance sectors.
- The B.B.A. (Banking & Finance) degree course covers the study of the basic concepts of management with specialization in the subjects such as International Banking and Finance, Treasury Operations, Risk Management, Investment Banking, Project & Infrastructure etc
- Some of the job types are:

  - o Assistant Controller
  - o Business Analyst
  - o Credit Analyst
  - o Financial Analyst
  - o Financial Consultant
  - o Finance Executive
  - o Financial Manager
  - o Finance Officer
  - o Internal Auditor
  - o Investment Analyst
  - o Loan Counsellor
  - o Loan Officer
  - o Marketing and Sales Executive
  - o Management Analyst
  - o Personal Financial Advisor
  - o Recovery Agent
  - o Research Analyst
  - o Tax Assistant
  - o Treasurer

Scope

- Banks
- Insurance Industry
- Charity Associations
- Business Schools
- Savings and Loan Associations
- Credit Unions

- Mortgage Companies
- Finance Companies
- Consultancies
- Shopping Malls

B.B.A. *Information Systems*
Area of work

- This course includes the study of using computer technologies to analyse business problems and processes in order to design and implement computer-based information systems which support business operations, decision-making and planning.
- Career opportunities exist in management consulting companies and in other industries mainly in the area of system development, database administration, network management and corporate information system management.

Scope

- Banks
- Insurance Industry
- Charity Associations
- Business Schools
- Savings and Loan Associations
- Credit Unions
- Mortgage Companies
- Finance Companies
- Consultancies
- Shopping Malls
- Management Consulting Firms
- Government Agencies
- Large and Small Corporations

B.B.A. *Marketing and Finance*
Area of work

- Marketing and finance is a challenging area that involves calculating and analysing the data and there are many KPIs, metrics and measurements involved in this.
- Some of the job types are:

    o   Marketing Management

o   Assignment Writer
o   Relationship Manager—Marketing & Finance
o   Marketing & Finance Executive
o   Finance & Marketing Controller
o   Business School Professor/Lecturer
o   Finance Controller

Scope

- Banks
- Insurance Industry
- Charity Associations
- Business Schools
- Savings and Loan Associations
- Credit Unions
- Mortgage Companies
- Finance Companies
- Consultancies
- Shopping Malls
- Management Consulting Firms
- Government Agencies
- Large and Small Corporations

B.B.A. *Retail Management*
Area of work

- Retail Management is a professional course to train individuals in various aspects of retailing
- Retailing involves a direct contact with customers and also involves the coordination of business activities beginning from the design stage of a product to its delivery and post-delivery service
- Retail businesses include:

    o   Factory outlets
    o   Specialty stores
    o   Supermarkets
    o   Franchisee
    o   Chain stores
    o   Discount stores
    o   Lifestyle & personal products
    o   Furnishing & house hold appliances

Scope

- Banks
- Insurance Industry
- Charity Associations
- Business Schools
- Credit Unions
- Mortgage Companies
- Finance Companies
- Consultancies
- Shopping Malls
- Management Consulting Firms
- Government Agencies
- Large and Small Corporations
- Automobile Industry
- Aviation Industry

B.B.A./B.Com. International Business
Area of work

- This course aims at providing a detailed study of all the important areas and disciplines relevant to international business activities

Scope

- Banks
- Insurance Industry
- Charity Associations
- Business Schools
- Savings and Loan Associations
- Credit Unions
- Mortgage Companies
- Finance Companies
- Consultancies
- Shopping Malls
- Management Consulting Firms
- Government Agencies
- Large and Small Corporations
- Automobile Industry
- Aviation Industry
- Credit Companies
- Health Departments

- Property Developers
- Research Agencies

B.B.S. or Bachelor of Business Studies
Area of work

- Business Studies is a study in the fields of accountancy, finance, marketing, organizational studies and economics
- Some of the job types are:

  o Teaching
  o Manager
  o Consultant
  o Business Analyst-Analysing
  o Junior Accountant
  o Business Development Manager
  o Business analyst

Scope

- Corporate Sector
- Accounting
- Marketing
- Finance
- Project Management
- Relationship Management
- Professional Occupations

B.C.A (Bachelor of Computer Applications)
Area of work

- Someone can pursue a Bachelor degree in Computers Application (BCA) followed by an MBA (Master in Business Administration) or an MCA (Master in Computer Applications) to make a career in the field of IT (Information Technology).
- Some of the job types are:

  o Teacher/lecturer
  o Business Consultants
  o Chief Information Officer
  o Computer Programmer
  o Computer Trainer

- o Computer System Analyst
- o Computer Scientist
- o Computer Support Service Specialist
- o Computer Presentation Specialist
- o Commercial and Industrial Designer
- o Database Administrator
- o Independent Consultant
- o Information System Manager
- o Project Manager
- o Systems Administrator
- o Software Developer
- o Software Publisher

Scope

- Banks, Insurance Companies and other financial institutions
- Colleges/Universities
- Multi-National Companies
- IT professionals are required in almost all sectors of business

B.Com

Area of work

- Subjects include Business Studies, Economics, Banking & Finance, Accounting and Auditing & Taxation etc.
- Some of the job types are:

  - o Accounts Assistant
  - o Assistant Accountant
  - o Accountant
  - o Business Analyst
  - o Cashier/Teller
  - o Corporate Analyst
  - o Executive Assistant
  - o Finance Manager
  - o Financial Analyst
  - o Investments Analyst
  - o Investment Banker
  - o Market Analyst
  - o Marketing Manager
  - o Money Manager
  - o Operations Manager

o Personal Finance Consultant
o Risk Analyst
o Securities Analyst
o Senior Accountant

Scope

- Various Corporate Sectors in their Marketing and Accounts Sections
- Finance, Commerce and the Banking Sectors
- Research Associates with Economic Consulting Firms
- Economic Consulting Jobs
- Customs Department
- Import/Export Companies

B.Com. (Business Economics and Business Environment)
Area of work

- This course includes the study of economic issues and problems related to business organization, management and strategy.

Scope

- Banks
- Accountancy, Administrative Offices, Tax Advisors
- Consultancy
- General Public Administration
- Economic Research/Consultancy Firms
- Trade (Particularly Wholesale Companies) and Multinationals
- Entrepreneurship

B.Com. (Business Mathematics and Statistics)
Area of work

- The aim of the program is to educate graduates with developed mathematical, statistical and computational skills with the ability to apply them to a quantitative analysis of industrial, commercial or financial business decisions.
- Some of the job types are:

o Account Executive
o Accountant
o Actuary

- o Banker
- o Banking and Finance Professional
- o Business Analyst
- o Certified Practicing Accountant
- o Computer Game Programmer
- o Corporate Secretary
- o Economist
- o Financial Advisor/Analyst
- o Financial Project Manager
- o Funds Manager
- o Government Officer
- o Investment Manager
- o Market Research Manager
- o Mathematician
- o Quantitative Analyst
- o Risk Manager
- o Statistician
- o Stockbroker

Scope

- Banks, Insurance Companies

B.Com. (Commercial Law)
Area of work

- Commercial Law or Business Law cover most aspects of the business spectrum, including management and operations, accounting, bookkeeping and financing, bankruptcy, contracts, sales, marketing and commerce, buying and selling business entities and their components, labour relations and taxes.

Scope

- Legal practice
- Government
- Politics
- The media
- Parliament or legislature
- Merchant banking
- International business
- Money markets

B.Com. (Honours)
Area of work

- B.Com. (Honours) is a graduate degree program that focuses on the systematic study of the concepts of Accountancy, Business Studies, Statistics, Economics, Mathematics, Finance, Banking, Law, Taxation, Marketing, Management Studies etc
- Some of the job types are:
  - Assistant Accountant
  - Accountant
  - Business Analyst
  - Cashier/Teller
  - Corporate Analyst
  - Executive Assistant
  - Finance Manager
  - Financial Analysts
  - Investments Analyst
  - Investment Banker
  - Market Analysts
  - Marketing Manager
  - Money Manager
  - Operations Manager
  - Personal Finance Consultant
  - Risk Analyst
  - Securities Analyst
  - Senior Accountant

Scope

- Various Corporate Sectors in their Marketing and Accounts Sections
- Finance, Commerce and the Banking Sectors
- Research Associates with Economic Consulting Firms
- Economic Consulting Jobs
- Customs Department
- Import/Export Companies

B.Com. Accounting & Taxation
Area of work

- The study of accounting & taxation includes Tax System, Financial Accounting, Principles of Management, Value Added Tax and

Central Tax Procedure, Financial Accounting and Business Communication.

- Some of the job types are:

  o Accountant
  o Revenue Agent
  o Marketing Manager
  o Financial Analyst
  o Tax Policy Analyst
  o Employment Tax Specialist
  o Personal Finance Consultant
  o Assistant Manager-Taxation
  o Senior Executive Taxation
  o Executive Indirect Taxation
  o Accountant-Indirect Taxation
  o Head-Corporate Taxation

Scope

- Tax
- Audit
- Financial
- Budget Analysis
- Corporate Finance
- Real Estate Finance
- International Finance
- Management Accounting

B.Com. Actuarial Management
Area of work

- Actuarial science is the discipline that applies mathematical and statistical methods to assess risk in the insurance and finance industries. Actuarial science includes a number of inter-related subjects including probability, mathematics, statistics, finance, economics, financial economics and computer programming
- Some of the job types are:

  o Life Actuarial Senior Associate
  o Actuarial Programmer
  o Actuarial Analyst
  o Actuarial Science Tutor/Teacher
  o Property and Casualty Actuarial Manager

o Assistant Professor in Actuarial Sciences
o Analyst Actuarial Services
o Health and Benefits Actuarial Consultant
o Actuarial Manager
o Actuarial Analyst

Scope

- Banks

B.Com. Advertising & Brand Management
Area of work

- The course includes the practical exposure and theoretical concepts about advertising and brand management.
- Some of the job types are:

    o Brand Manager
    o Trade Marketing Manager
    o Customer Development Officer
    o Instrument Operator
    o Assistant Mechanic
    o Brand Activation & Customer Relationship Marketing Specialist
    o Marketing Manager
    o Publishing Manager
    o Product Development Manager
    o Area Sales Manager
    o Teacher & Lecturer
    o Advertising and Brand Manager
    o Assistant Brand Manager
    o Product/Brand Manager

Scope

- Companies

B.Com. Applied Business Accounting
Area of work

- Students of this course have more opportunities in their career to get elevated to the level as Finance Manager, Finance Advisor,

Business Advisor, Finance Controller, and Finance Director in India and in abroad
- Some of the job types are:

  o   B.Com. Accountancy Job Types
  o   Finance Managers
  o   Financial Advisors
  o   Directors (Finance)
  o   Financial Controllers
  o   Chief Financial Officer
  o   Certified Public Accountant
  o   Chartered Management Accountant

Scope

- Banks

B.Com. Applied Economics
Area of work

- Applied Economics deals with the application of economic analysis to specific problems in both the public and private sectors. It brings up the quantitative studies, the results of which are of use in the practical field, and thus helps to bring economic theory nearer to reality.
- Some of the job types are:

  o   Statistician
  o   Assistant Manager/Officer
  o   Statistical Assistant
  o   Service Quality Leader
  o   Market Research Analyst
  o   Lead Modeller
  o   Economics Teacher
  o   Curriculum Developer
  o   Subject Matter Experts-Economics
  o   Data Analyst-Energy Economics

Scope

- Banks
- Companies

B.Com. Banking and Finance
Area of work

- This course generally covers the study of the concepts of Banking, Accounting, Banking Law and Insurance Law.
- Some of the job types are:

  o   Actuary
  o   Accountant
  o   Administrative Officer (AO)
  o   Agent and Broker
  o   Asset Manager
  o   Assistant Accountant
  o   Assistant Administrative Officer (AAO)
  o   Assistant Controller
  o   Cashier/Teller
  o   Credit and Risk Manager
  o   Customer Service Representative
  o   Development Officer
  o   Equity Research Analyst
  o   Internal Auditor
  o   Insurance Manager
  o   Investment Analyst
  o   Investment Banker
  o   Loan Counsellor
  o   Loss Control Specialist
  o   Loan Officer
  o   Market Analyst
  o   Marketing and Sales Executive
  o   Marketing Manager
  o   Personal Financial Advisor
  o   Recovery Agent
  o   Risk Analyst
  o   Sales Representative

Scope

- Automobile Industry
- Aviation Industry
- Banks
- Business Schools
- Charity Associations

- Consultancies
- Credit Companies
- Educational Institutes
- Economic Consulting Jobs
- Health Departments
- Indian Civil Services
- Indian Economic Services
- Insurance Industry
- Investments
- Mortgage Companies
- Property Developers
- Research Agencies
- Research Associates with Economic Consulting Firms
- Savings and Loan Associations

B.Com. Computer Applications
Area of work

- Some of the job types are:

  o Mobile Application Developer
  o CAD Application Support Technician
  o Asst. Prof./Associate Prof./Professor-Computer Applications
  o Computer Application Specialist and Accounts Assistant
  o Computer Programmer
  o Computer Operator
  o Computer Assistant
  o Applications Developer (Informatics)
  o Computer-Laboratory Technician
  o Computer Scientist/Member Technical Staff
  o Clerk-Cum-Computer Operator

Scope

- Companies

B.Com. Corporate Secretary-ship
Area of work

- Calling meetings, recording minutes of the meetings, keeping statutory record books, proper payment of dividend and interest payments, and proper drafting and execution of agreements, contracts, and resolutions, etc.

- Some of the job types are:

  o Manager Corporate/Institutional Sales
  o Head-Corporate Development
  o Manager-corporate communications
  o Corporate Sales Executive
  o Corporate Sales Officer
  o Corporate Credit Analyst
  o Corporate Financial Analyst
  o Manager-Corporate Services
  o Company Secretary
  o Head-Finance & Administration
  o Export Manager

Scope

- Bank

B. Com. E-Commerce
Area of work

- Focus on the technology and online business practices of a company
- Automatic information system to conduct business on the Internet

Scope

- E-commerce Developer
- Web Consultant
- Business Analyst
- Business Solutions Manager
- E-commerce Consultant
- Executive-E-commerce
- E-Commerce-Project Coordinator
- E-Commerce Operations Manager (Technical)
- Business development-Senior Manage
- Trainee E-commerce
- E-Commerce Product Sales Manager
- E commerce-Business Analyst

B.Com. Foreign Trade Management
Area of work

- Offer a global perspective and help build a solid foundation and understanding of the factors affecting the global marketplace
- Some of the job types are:

  - o Merchandiser
  - o Financial Analyst
  - o Investments Analyst
  - o Corporate Analyst
  - o Accountant, Tax Advisor
  - o Market Analyst
  - o Business Analyst
  - o Equity Research Analyst
  - o Marketing Manager
  - o Investment Banker
  - o Operations Manager
  - o Budget Analyst
  - o Auditor
  - o Revenue Agent
  - o Personal Finance Consultant

Scope

- International finance
- Export marketing firms
- Pre-shipment and post-shipment quality control labs
- Banks and financial institutions
- Directorate general of foreign trade
- Shipping companies/corporations
- Marine insurance companies
- State trading corporations
- Transportation corporations
- Logistic companies
- Dry ports, ports
- Special economic zones
- Custom clearing houses

B.Com. Information Technology
Area of work

- In this technologically advanced world, no business can run without a solid IT support. The bigger a business, the more extensive is its IT support.
- Manage planning, design, selection, implementation, usage & administration of emerging and converging information & communications technologies
- Some of the job types are:
    o 3D Animation & Graphic Designer
    o Customer Service
    o Programmer & Software Developer
    o Quality Assurance (QA), System Analyst & Tester
    o Technical Support (Technician & Help Desk)
    o Security Expert
    o Computer Operator
    o Technical Assistant-Computer
    o Computer Assistant
    o Computer Programmer
    o Computer Teacher

Scope

- Multi-National Companies
- Banks and other financial institutions
- Colleges and universities

B.Com. Office Management
Area of work

- Open, sort and distribute incoming mail, and collect, seal and stamp outgoing mail
- Deliver oral or written messages
- Collect and distribute paperwork, such as records or timecards from one department to another
- Mark, tabulate and file articles and records
- May deliver items to other business establishments
- May deliver stock certificates and bonds within and between stock brokerage offices and be designated Runner

Scope

- Office Assistant
- Office Secretary
- Human Resource Team
- Office automation jobs in Govt/Public/Private sectors

Chartered Accountant
Area of work

- Chartered accountancy is primarily about accounting, auditing and taxation.
- A chartered accountant is trained in various aspects of finance and accounting
- Help companies and individuals in tax planning and compliance.

Scope

- Multi-National Companies
- Banks and other financial institutions
- Colleges and universities

Company Secretary (CS)
Area of work

- A Company Secretary (CS) ensures a company's legal & regulatory compliance and guides the board of the company on governance issues.
- Guide the board on shareholders meetings, meetings of directors
- Establish a link between the board & stakeholders like shareholders, deposit holders, stock exchanges & regulators
- Some of the job roles are:

    o   Arbitration and Conciliation
    o   Capital Market and Investor Relations
    o   Corporate Advisory Services
    o   Corporate Restructuring
    o   Due Diligence
    o   Foreign Collaborations and Joint Ventures
    o   Financial Management
    o   Legal, Secretarial and Corporate Governance
    o   Project Planning

Scope

- Banks
- Company Law Boards
- Company Secretary Ship Consultancy Firms
- Departments of Company Affairs
- Financial Institutions
- Government Departments
- Other Regulatory Bodies
- Private Companies
- Stock Exchanges

Cost and Work Accountant (CWA)
Area of work

- Collect, assimilate, collate & analyse all financial information of a company
- Some of the job types are:

  o Chief Accountant
  o Chief Internal Auditor
  o Cost and Management Accountant
  o Cost Consultant
  o Cost Controller
  o Finance Director
  o Financial Consultant
  o Financial Controller
  o Managing Director
  o Marketing Manager
  o Teacher

Scope

- Banks
- Company Law Boards
- Consultancy Firms
- Departments of Company Affairs
- Developmental Agencies
- Education Sector
- Financial Institutions
- Government Departments
- Private Companies

- Public Utility Sector
- Service Industry
- Stock Exchanges
- Training & Research Organizations

Diploma in Entrepreneurship
Area of work

- Help you develop the skills required to evaluate new & viable business opportunities, create new ventures & cultivate innovation
- Some of the job types are:

  - Trainee Telesales
  - Asst. Manager-Costing
  - Chief Human Resources Officer
  - Executive/Office Assistant
  - Senior Network Administrator
  - System Analyst-Build Configuration Management
  - Delivery Manager
  - Assistant Manager-Training Division
  - Trainee-Human Capital Management
  - Head-Entrepreneurship
  - Recruitment-Marketing Executive
  - Placement Coordinator
  - Finance Controller

Scope

- Multi-National Companies
- Banks and other financial institutions
- Colleges and universities

Diploma in Human Resources
Area of work

- Recruitment, training, team building, performance updates, employee policy, salary, benefits and increments, employee health and safety as well as staff amenities
- Some of the job types are:

  - Assistant Manager-Human Resource Management

o   Professor-Human Resource Management
o   Human Resource Executive
o   Accountant-Human Resource Management
o   Production Officer-Human Resource Management
o   Domain Experts-Human Resources

Scope

- Multi-National Companies

Government Jobs

There are various government jobs available for graduates in various streams/specializations. There are competitive exams at various levels for these jobs. Some of the examples are UPSC exams, SSC exams, Bank jobs, Railway jobs, Teaching jobs and other government jobs. There are various exams conducted all the year for these jobs at state and centre level.

DECIDE WISELY

Make the decision, make it with confidence, and the world will be yours.
—Jaren L. Davis

Now you have a big list of career options available with you. The next step is to find out which option out of this list suits you. This step requires maturity and decision making capability. If you are good to take decisions, you can go ahead otherwise you can take help of your parents, teacher, any other mature person or a career guide for decision making.

Take 4-5 career options you like from the big list of options and then proceed to the steps mentioned here to choose the best out of them.

Know your personality

The first thing to look at is your personality. Your personality should match with the profession you are planning to choose. Take a paper and pen and note down the answers of following questions:

- Write down some details about yourself, your family, siblings, friends and other persons you spend time with. Mention about their character, likings, habits, and lifestyle and about the things that keep you attached with them.
- Write down some details on how you are grown up. Also mention about the good and bad experiences of your childhood.
- Write about the things you like and dislike and reasons for this.
- Write about the habits you like and dislike and the reasons for this.
- Write about the persons you like and dislike and the reasons for this.
- What makes you feel happy or sad? And why?
- How is your current lifestyle and how is the lifestyle that you want to adopt in future?
- Are there any mis-happenings, bad memories or tragic moments in your life that you can't forget and what is their impact on your life?
- What are your hobbies and favourite time pass?

- How much are your family income and how much of it can be spent for your career?
- How is your social life?
- Do you like travelling?
- Do you have any preferences of work location?
- How is your physique?
- What about your health and body fitness?
- Do you or your family have any special needs or expectations from your career?
- Do you have any special god gifted talents?
- What are your personal values?
- What are your priorities in your life?
- How much you can sacrifice for your career?

Once you are done with this, read all this 2-3 times. This will give you a picture about whether your opted career option is suitable for you or not.

Evaluate your skills

The world is all full of opportunities and you are full of skills and talents. The almighty God has not created anything useless in this world. Therefore, never under-estimate yourself and always try to find the special god gifted talents in you. Give some time to discover yourself, know your skills and abilities and then decide your future career path.

1. Analytical Skills

These skills can be judged as:

- Ability of a person to gather and analyse information applying logical thinking
- Ability of a person to visualize, describe, and solve problems based on the information gathered
- Ability of a person to make decisions based on available information
- Ability of a person to design and test solutions to problems
- Ability of a person to formulate plans
- Ability of a person to see the arguments on both sides of an issue, and being able to analyse the merits of each argument

Suitable career options for those having good analytical skills are: Legal profession, System analyst, Business analyst, Psychologist, Stock market

2. Behavioural Skills

These skills can be judged as:

- Making efforts for personal development
- Trying to resolve problems on personal responsibility
- Understanding the way people really feel
- Developing positive relationships
- Reliable and dependable
- Managing stress and conflicts
- Managing managerial superiors and peers
- Contributing positively to team/company
- Seeking and picking up responsibility
- Having compassion and care for others

Suitable career options for those having good behavioural skills are: Sales and Marketing, Human relations, Consultancy head

3. Business Skills

These skills can be judged as:

- Public speaking skills
- Sales and Marketing skills
- Strategic skills
- Risk mitigation skills
- Time management and stress management skills
- Leadership skills
- Imagination and creativity
- Problem solving skills

Suitable career options for those having good business skills are: Entrepreneurship, Business handling, Business administration and management

4. Mathematical Skills

These skills can be judged as:

- Reasoning Ability
- Ability to manipulate ideas about understanding of a concept in a variety of ways

- Recognize, interpret, and apply the signs, symbols and terms used to represent concepts
- Compare, contrast and integrate related concepts and principles
- Know and apply facts and definitions
- Identify and apply principles
- Use and interrelate models and diagrams

Suitable career options for those having good mathematical skills are: Scientific design and development, Management services and computing, Banking and finance, Statistical work, Teaching

5. General Knowledge

These skills can be judged as:

- Culturally valued knowledge communicated by a range of non-specialist media and encompassing a wide subject range
- Excludes highly specialized learning that can only be obtained with extensive training and information
- 20 domains of knowledge that meet the above criteria: Art, Biology, Classical music, Cookery, Discovery and exploration, Fashion, Film, Finance, Games, General science, Geography, History, History of science, Literature, Medicine, Music, Politics, Popular music, Sport, Television
- 20 domains could be categorised into six factors: Current affairs, fashion, family, physical health and recreation, arts, and science

Suitable career options for those having good general knowledge are: Required in many government and private exams and also in exams for foreign studies

6. Presentation Skills

These skills can be judged as:

- Able to present information clearly and effectively
- Able to talk to a group of people, addressing a meeting or briefing a team

Suitable career options for those having good presentation skills are: Video conferencing executive, Sales and marketing, Workshop coordinators for companies, Tele-conferencing expert

7. Research Skills

These skills can be judged as:

- Ability of a person to search some fact carefully to answer a question
- It is wider than finding out a fact and more focused than reading widely around a subject.

Suitable career options for those having good research skills are: Historians, Editors, Law teachers, Educational jobs, Chief executives

8. Teaching Skills

These skills can be judged as:

- Able to create a comfortable learning environment
- Able to prepare, organize and deliver study material
- Able to understand needs of the students
- Able to set goals and expectations

Suitable career options for those having good presentation skills are: Teacher, Lecturer

Judge your attitude

Your attitude decides, how much successful you can be, in your career. Some of the attributes to judge your attitude are:

1. Patience

This attribute can be understood as:

- Power of enduring an unpleasant or difficult process or situation without giving away, which can mean persevering in the face of delay or provocation without acting on annoyance/anger in a negative way
- Exhibiting tolerance when under strain or when faced with longer-term difficulties

2. Customer Service

This attribute can be understood as anticipating, meeting and/or exceeding customer needs and expectations.

3. Continuous Learning

This attribute can be understood as:

- Taking initiative in learning and implementing new concepts, technologies and/or methods for learning
- Listen for positive attitude towards self-improvement, learning and the application of knowledge

4. Self-Management

- Demonstrating self-control and ability to manage time and priorities
- Listen for composure, assertiveness and emotional stability

5. Team-work

This attribute can be understood as:

- Working effectively and productively with others
- Listen for strong commitment and contributions to team members working towards a specific goal

6. Interpersonal skills

This attribute can be understood as:

- Effectively communicating, building rapport and relating well to all kinds of people
- Listen for self-awareness, understanding and an ability to communicate effectively with others regardless of differences

7. Goal Orientation

This attribute can be understood as:

- Energetically focusing efforts on meeting a goal, mission or objective
- Listen for determination, persistence and a "never-give-up" attitude in efforts to meet goals

8. Empathy

This attribute can be understood as:

- Identifying with and caring about others
- Listen for genuine caring, compassion and initiative in assisting others without expectations of rewards

9. Honesty

This attribute can be understood as:

- Honesty refers to integrity, truthfulness and straight forwardness
- Honesty means being truthful, trustworthy, loyal, fair and sincere

10. Integrity

This attribute can be understood as:

- Integrity is a concept of consistency of actions, values, methods, measures, principles, expectations, and outcomes
- In ethics, integrity is regarded as the honesty and truthfulness or accuracy of one's actions
- Integrity is the inner sense of "wholeness" deriving from qualities such as honesty and consistency of character

11. Reliability

This attribute can be understood as:

- Reliability is the ability of a person to perform and maintain its functions in routine circumstances, as well as hostile or unexpected circumstances.

12. Accuracy

This attribute can be understood as the ability of a person to do some work or perform some task correctly and accurately with minimum or no errors or mistakes.

Discover your interests

All that matters is your interest. If you have all the skills and talents required for a career option but you do not have an interest in that field, I suggest not go for that. If you have a strong interest in some field and you do not have the skills required for that career option, you can work hard and try to develop those skills.

You can ask yourself the question like, which of the following work makes you happy, to find the options where your interest lies:

- Advising other people
- Cars, Trucks or other vehicles
- Clothes or textiles
- Contributing to people's health and well-being
- Controlling and monitoring equipment and technology
- Creating original works of art
- Designing buildings and structures
- Developing new ideas or solutions
- Diagnosing and treating patients
- Diet and nutrition
- Drawing plans, maps and charts
- Driving vehicles or heavy machinery
- Electronics, electrical or telecommunication systems
- Finding the quality of information, products or services
- Food and drink
- Government policies and decisions
- Hair, beauty and personal appearance
- Installing, repairing and maintaining equipment and technology
- Interviewing people for information
- Making calculations
- Managing information
- Managing or supervising people
- Painting, decorating or coating objects
- Performing drama, play, stage show
- Pet grooming and care
- Physical activity
- Planning or organising activities
- Protecting nature and the environment
- Providing customer service to people
- Providing people with support, counselling and guidance
- Providing personal care to people
- Researching or analysing information
- Selling, promoting or trading
- Speaking or studying languages
- Sport and recreation
- Studying societies and cultures
- Teaching people how to do things
- Understanding human behaviour
- Understanding law

PLAN TO WIN

You were born to win, but to be a winner, you must plan to win,
prepare to win, and expect to win.—Zig Ziglar

Once you decide the career option suitable for you, the next step is to make a plan to successfully achieve it. There are few things that you should take care of while planning for your career.

Make short term and long term goals

Decide about the career, you are opting for, as early as possible. This will give you enough time to prepare and successfully achieve your target. Once you decide finally about the career field, take a pen and notebook, and write down the answers to the following questions:

What is the minimum qualification required for the career you opted for?

How much time you have with you, to achieve the minimum qualification required for this career choice?

Are there any entrance exams or other test you have to qualify after the minimum qualification?

Is there any interview or group discussion involved?

What are the required skills?

Do you have these skills or you need learning and development programs?

Are you aware about the institutions that provide the learning programs on skills where you lack?

Now make a plan to plan the activities involved (Study, Entrance Test, Other Exams, Interviews, Group Discussions, and Skills Development) according to the time you have with you.

Make short term as well as long term goals to complete the activities on time.

Timely review your progress

Take a close look of the goal sheet you prepared 2-3 times. Make some reminders about the time frame decided to accomplish various short term and long term goals. You must observe your progress weekly on every Sunday and write the following details for every goal on a notepad.

What have you done this week to accomplish this short term or long term goal?

Is the work done on this goal, during this week, sufficient to accomplish this goal within specified time frame?

Are you facing any difficulties or problems to work on this goal?

If there are any difficulties you are facing to work on a goal, how are you going to solve these problems?

Do you require any external help? If yes, whom?

Do you think you will be able to accomplish this goal within specified time frame?

After looking into the answers of these questions, you will be able to judge where you stand on your career path.

Be fast and try to complete your goals within specified timeframe.

Take help from others, wherever required.

Never delay anything related to your goals.

Never forget to review your progress.

Come on the dance floor

The famous saying is—Opportunity dances with those already on the dance floor. It means you should be ready with all your preparations to grab the opportunity when it comes.